Early American Wars

Texas War of Independence

Robert O'Neill, Series Editor; and Alan C. Huffines

This edition published in 2011 by:

The Rosen Publishing Group, Inc.
29 East 21st Street
New York, NY 10010

Library of Congress Cataloging-in-Publication Data

Huffines, Alan C.
Texas war of independence / Alan C. Huffines.
    p. cm.—(Early American wars)
Includes bibliographical references and index.
ISBN 978-1-4488-1332-2 (library binding)
1. Texas—History—Revolution, 1835–1836. 2. Texas—History—To 1846. 3. Southwest, New—History—To 1848. 4. Mexican War, 1846–1848. I. Title.
F390.H925 2011
976.4'03—dc22

                                                                    2010030842

Manufactured in the United States of America

CPSIA Compliance Information: Batch #W11YA: For further information, contact Rosen Publishing, New York, New York, at 1-800-237-9932.

On the cover: *The Battle of San Jacinto* by Henry Arthur McArdle. (Texas State Library and Archives Commission)

Contents

Introduction 5

Chronology 12

Background to war
Mexican revolutions 17

Warring sides
The "Army of the People" faces the "Napoleon of the West" 24

Outbreak
"Come and take it" 31

The fighting
"Victory or Death" 37

Portrait of a soldier
Juan Almonte 60

The world around the war
The Jacksonian era 65

Portrait of a civilian
Angelina Dickenson, "Babe of the Alamo" 71

How the war ended
"Take them dead Mexicans off my league" 75

Conclusion and consequences
Independence and annexation 82

Glossary 89
For more information 90
For further reading 92
Index 93

Introduction

"This country should be given back to nature and the Indians."

Marqués de Rubíl (1766)

In many respects it was a European civil war: the descendants of northern European Protestants fought and defeated the offspring of southern European Catholics in a seven-month war of independence. The age-old challenges of European hegemony were exposed in the Mexican province of Texas. Removed by an ocean (and often several generations) from their ancestral homelands, each side nonetheless fought each other with a hatred and vigilance that made this war seem as feudal as the many past wars fought over similar interests, so long before and so far away. The former colonists of northern

Texas and Mexico 1830

1. The Sabine River acted as the immigrants' entry point from the U.S.
2. The Nueces formed the southern border of Texas from 1824–36.
3. Part of El Camino Reale (Old San Antonio Road)

Texas as part of Mexico 1824.

The earliest known daguerreotype of the Alamo, taken from just south of the eastern corner of the gate (*galera*), in the late 1840s before the U.S. Army "taco-belled" it. Just on the right side of the church is the *convento* connecting wall. Nothing remains of the palisade that connected the *galera* to the church. (Center for American History, The University of Texas at Austin)

and southern Europe, each with competing political, economic, cultural and religious ideals, struggled over control of the North American continent. The land could not be shared but must be conquered by one or the other.

The Viceroyalty of New Spain

The Spanish Crown had laid claim to the North American continent north and west of the Río Grande since the 16th century, and a large portion of that area (265,000 square miles [686,347 sq km]) would become Texas. The name Tejas, or Texas, came from Caddo vernacular meaning "friendly." As the Aztec influence became stronger in the Viceroyalty of New Spain (especially after Mexican

independence in 1821), the "j" would be dropped and replaced with the Aztec "x."

In 1528 Spanish accountant and conquistador Álvar Núñez (Cabeza de Vaca) was shipwrecked off the coast of Texas and wandered the Great Plains for eight years, finally encountering his countrymen again in 1536. He made his way to Mexico City in that year with vastly exaggerated tales of his travels that gave rise to the legends of the "Seven Golden cities of Cibola." He was soon followed by the conquistadors Francisco Vásquez de Coronado (1510–54) and Juan de Oñate (*c.* 1550–1630), who explored the "new" area of the viceroyalty (just as Francisco Pizarro and Hernando Cortés did further south) for the Church, for the king, and to bring the message of Christ to the savages of the region. Despite trekking through Texas, Oklahoma, and as far north as present-day Kansas, Coronado found no gold. The Spaniards persisted in the search, however, and spared no expense in the effort to locate these great treasures—after all who could make better use of golden cities, Spain, or the aborigines who had no concept of what worth gold held? The cities certainly existed, but they were not made of gold—they were the *pueblo* of the Zuñi tribe (situated in present-day western New Mexico).

The Spaniards never meant to colonize the region, at least not in the same way as their northern European neighbors understood the term. They intended to incorporate Mexico as a province of Spain, to use the land and its inhabitants through a series of land ventures called *encomienda* and *estancia de ganado* (cattle ranches). Drawn by the prospect of cheap land and great wealth, Spanish adventurers continued to travel to the New World, and by 1600 there were a quarter of a million Spaniards in the Americas. The Spaniards claimed title to the land and used the indigenous population as labor. The *encomienda* ended in 1720 and left in its wake a peculiar caste system of landowner and laborer that would continue to haunt Mexico throughout its maturity.

The Texas mission period began in 1690 with the founding of the Mission San Francisco de los Tejas in east Texas by Franciscan monks. When compared to the Jesuits, who were attempting to accomplish the same task in Canada and Central America, the Franciscan order was possibly the more disciplined and intent of the two. Catholic missions were established in Tejas (to include five in San Antonio), and stretched from Nagodoches to San Antonio and into El Paso. One of them, the Mission San Antonio de Valero was founded in 1718 and would arguably have the most colorful history of all these institutions.

In 1727 the Spanish colony north of Mexico became the province of Texas. There were several reasons (apart from Catholicism) for the missions and colonization, the most urgent being the need to arrest growing French exploration of east Texas. Another reason was historical legacy. By the 18th century Spain was declining as a culture and as an empire, and perhaps the only way to regain power and prestige in the global community was in the Viceroyalty of New Spain. At any rate, the Spaniards' policy of colonization became more traditional during the mission period, even more so when the first colonists arrived in 1731. Fifteen families from the Canary Islands arrived in San Antonio, chosen because of their hardiness and acclimatization to a harsh environment, and because Spaniards from the mainland did not want to colonize this particular outpost of the New World.

Early Native American disinterest in the Spaniards and their religion meant that colonization of this northern province seemed fragile. Plan after plan failed to bring in any large numbers of converts, and settlements were limited to small ecclesiastical missions, military bases (*presidios*), and civil outposts (*pueblos*). Not all the tribes were apathetic, however: the Comanche and Apache worked hard to destroy the settlements completely. Both of these nations carried on an extensive guerrilla war against Spain, and countless friars and *soldados* gave up.

Hostile natives were not the sole problem. The entire mission structure suffered from wholesale abuse of government finances and assets, from the challenges presented by a generally harsh climate, and from insufficient numbers of *soldados* and equipment. By the late 18th century, the *soldado de cuera* ("leather-jacketed soldier") who manned the isolated stations was still wearing leather armor and carrying a shield and lance to defend himself—similar equipment to that of their enemies, but hopelessly outdated in comparison to their European contemporaries. The main difference was that the French-sponsored Comanche and Apache were more numerous, better mounted and more motivated.

France ceded Louisiana to Spain in 1763 as a result of their alliance during the Seven Years War, which stopped French encroachment into Tejas. (Louisiana returned to French possession in 1800.) In 1766 Spain sent the Marqués de Rubí to tour the region and make recommendations for the dispersal of the land. He recommended that all missions and *presidios* (garrisons), except for those in San Antonio de Béxar and La Bahía (90 miles [145 km] east of Béxar) be

The *soldados de Cuera* ("leather-coated soldiers"), were the police of New Spain. They spent many years patrolling the frontier and often took Indian wives. Rarely regarded as part of the regular military establishment, they were ill-equipped and never organized above company level. When war came between Texas and Mexico, they sided with their mother country. (Archivo General de Indias, Seville)

dismantled and abandoned. He suggested that all colonists in Texas be relocated to San Antonio. Spain had conquered the Aztec, Maya and Inca Empires, yet could not destroy or even defend its property against two relatively small nomadic bands. The Comanche and Apache had defeated Spain: Texan colonization would have to wait.

After 75 years of operation, the Mission San Antonio de Valero could only document 43 converts, and in 1793 the Church secularized it. The property was distributed to the 13 remaining convert families, descendants of the original Canary Islanders. In 1801 a presidial "Flying Company," the Compañia Volante del Alamo de Parras, took over the former mission and converted the compound to a *presidio* (a "station of the garrison"). With the new occupants came a new name: Alamo.

At this time, the total population of colonists in Tejas numbered less than 3,000.

Revolution

The long struggle for the Viceroyalty's independence from Spain began in Dolores, Mexico, in 1810. Father Miguel Hidalgo y Costilla, a Catholic priest, raised his *grito* (shout of revolt), "Death to Spaniards!" against the monarchy. The causes had little to do with liberties or republican ideals, but were more concerned with social and class divisions, as well as land redistribution.

The society of New Spain was organized around ethnic groupings. The governing and priestly classes were either native-born Spaniards or Spaniards born in Mexico (*creolos*). As in the United States, there was no identifiable middle class; close to the bottom of the social hierarchy were the *mestizos*, mixed-race descendants of Spaniards and Indians, who formed the bulk of Hidalgo's followers and made up about 80 percent of the population. The indigenous Indian population, who frequently did not

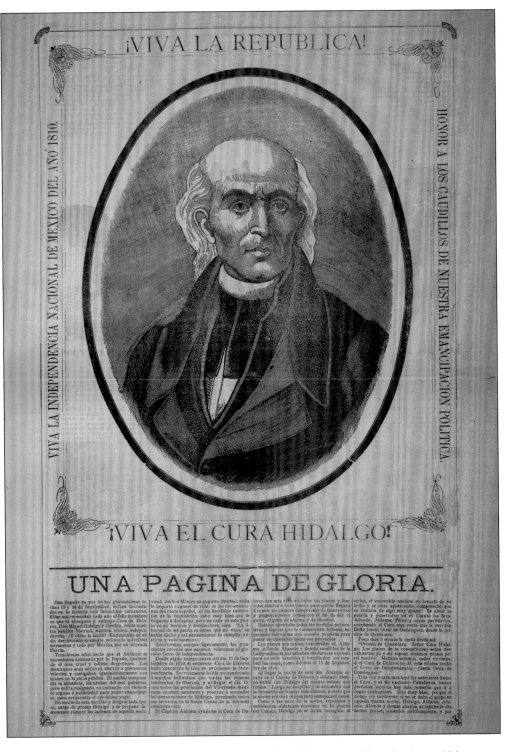

This broadsheet from the end of the 19th century celebrates Mexican independence by reminding its readers of the sacrifice and fervor of Mexico's earliest republican revolutionary, Father Miguel Hidalgo. The text reads, "Long live the republic! Long live Father Hidalgo! A page of glory!" (Library of Congress Prints and Photographs division LC-USZ62-98851)

The execution of Father José María Morelos. Royalist forces executed Almonte's father as a revolutionary leader on December 22, 1815. He is seen kneeling, blindfolded and holding a crucifix. (From *Album Pintoresco de la Republica Mexicana*, 1848)

practice Catholicism or speak Spanish, were at the bottom of the social pyramid.

Hidalgo captured several cities and provinces: Guanajuato, Guadalajara, Nuevo Santander and Coahuila. Because the revolution was organized along social lines, the real power in New Spain—the landowners, Church and army—believed the revolt was aimed at them and gave their loyalty to Spain. Hidalgo's rebellion failed in less than a year, and he and a goodly portion of his subordinate leadership were captured and executed. But many of his followers who wanted a change in government escaped, and a bloody guerrilla war ensued.

Bernardo Gutiérrez de Lara, who represented the transition from simple class struggle to a war for republican values, evaded capture and fled to the United States, reaching Washington City on December 11, 1811. He clearly believed that he would secure support for Mexico's struggle against its colonial masters in this capital of republicanism. In correspondence with like-minded republicans, he became acquainted with Augustus Magee, an officer in the U.S. Army who had been assigned to guard the Texas–Louisiana border. Magee resigned his commission in January (no small event on the eve of the 1812 war with Great Britain), and went about raising the "Republican Army of the North" from volunteers in the United States.

Magee and Gutiérrez thought they were of the same mind. Immediately Gutiérrez took nominal command of the army (so as not to raise concern over an Anglo-led army of freebooters and border scum), with Magee as his deputy. Magee had soon assembled around 800 men, who, for the most part, were not pirates or ruffians looking for a fight, but held the same republican ideals as those espoused by Magee and Gutiérrez. Mexico's Republican Army of the North would invade and liberate Tejas.

Tejas was the logical place to begin. If the royalists were thrown out, and a republican state established, then Hidalgo's *grito* could again be raised in Mexico itself. The revolution would be reborn.

On August 7, 1812, the advance guard of the army crossed the Río Sabine into Spanish Tejas, and took up the march toward Nacogdoches. The tiny royalist garrison at this border town, *soldados* who checked duties and tariffs, fled. The first engagement went to the republicans. In response, the Spanish governor Manuel María de Salcedo sent 1,500 royalist *soldados* to meet them. The republicans outmaneuvered this force and captured Presidio La Bahía on November 7, 1812.

The royalists laid siege to the republicans ensconced behind La Bahía's stone walls. In February, Magee died. Another Anglo, Samuel Kemper, took command. The royalist besiegers took heavy casualties, and retired in March to San Antonio. The republicans followed and captured that town as well. All royalist forces in Tejas had been defeated and the republicans drafted a declaration of independence on April 6, 1813.

In the meantime, the deeds of the republican army had been told and retold in the United States. Fresh men began to find their way to San Antonio from across the Río Sabine. While earlier the republican army was "republican" in sentiment, the new recruits filtering in were freebooters, bandits, and adventurers, with no more interest in a republic than the royalists.

For the first time in this revolution, issues became parochial. The Anglo soldiers and leaders wanted Texas annexed to the United States. The Mexican leaders and *soldados* wanted Tejas to be a state in the future republic of Mexico. The followers of Gutiérrez won out and a *junta* took over and created a new constitution. Most of the Anglo-republicans went home. The Republican Army of the North numbered 3,000 *soldados*.

The royalists dispatched two armies bound for San Antonio to destroy the republicans. One army of 2,000 commanded by General Joaquín de Arredondo met the republicans on August 18, 1813. The following battle of the Medina was a bloodbath. The republican line held until their left flank collapsed and most of the republican force fled the field. Of the remaining Anglo-republicans, only 93 escaped. The royalists killed all the prisoners and wounded, then marched to San Antonio and executed 300 Béxareños suspected of republican sentiment, clearly demonstrating how Spain dealt with invaders and pirates. Arredondo's lieutenant on this occasion, one Antonio López de Santa Anna Perez de Lebron, learnt a great deal from the battle and its aftermath, which left a lasting impression on how to deal with treason and revolt.

Chronology

1810 **September 16:** Father Miguel Hidalgo voices his *grito* of revolution against Spanish rule.

1812 **August 7:** "Republican Army of the North" captures Nacogdoches.

1813 **April 1:** Republicans capture San Antonio.

April 17: 1st Texas Declaration of Independence.

August 18: Royalist army destroys republicans at the battle of the Medina. Survivors and 300 Béxareños are executed.

1819 **June:** Dr. James Long and small force capture Nacogdoches and proclaim Texas Independence (again).

1821 **February 24:** General Agustín de Iturbide issues his *Plan de Iguala*.

1827 **December 16:** Benjamin Edwards proclaims "Republic of Fredonia" in Nacogdoches.

1829 **January 28:** "Fredonians" flee Nacogdoches and cross the Río Sabine after Texian militia are mobilized.

March 4: Andrew Jackson becomes President of the United States.

1830 **January 1:** James Bowie leaves Thibodaux, Louisiana, for Nacogdoches.

April 6: "Law of April 6, 1830" is passed in Mexico to halt Anglo immigration.

1831 **May:** William Barret Travis arrives as a colonist in San Felipe de Austin.

1832 **May:** William B. Travis and Patrick C. Jack are arrested by the Mexican authorities.

June 13: Turtle Bayou Resolutions declaring for federalism and Santa Anna.

June 26: Battle of Velasco.

July 3: Travis and Jack are released.

1833 **February:** Santa Anna is elected as a federalist president with Gómez Farías as vice-president.

March 9: Monclova replaces Saltillo as capital of Coahuila y Texas.

April 1: Santa Anna retires to his ranch and leaves federalist Farías in charge.

October 2: Austin writes to the *ayuntamiento* of Béxar, urging a state to be formed and "... to have everything in readiness ..."

November 15: Mexican senate rescinds the Law of April 6.

December 2: Crockett returns to the U.S. Congress.

1834 **January 3:** Austin is arrested in Saltillo for pronouncing a *grito* against the Mexican republic.

March 31: General Antonio López de Santa Anna de Perez de Lebron becomes President of Mexico.

May 25: Santa Anna usurps power with the *Pronunciamento de Cuernavaca*.

June 5: Coahuila's Governor Viesca, is arrested by centralists.

June 27: Travis and militia captures the centralist's Anahuac garrison and artillery to liberate Governor Viesca.

1835 **January 4:** A new Mexican congress is convened with a majority of cleric–military members. They elect General Miguel Barragán as the new vice-president.

March 31: All state militias are discharged. Zacatecas revolts.

May 10–11: Centralist forces kill 2,000 federalist rebels in Zacatecas, Mexico.

September 1: Austin returns to Texas from Mexico.

September 21: Centralist General Martín Perfecto de Cós lands at

Comanche Chief by Theodore Gentilz, (n.d.) The Comanche tribe was the most deadly foe the Spaniards, Mexicans and Texians faced throughout the early years of Texas, and remained a threat to settlers until 1874. (Courtesy of Béxar County and the Witte Museum, San Antonio, Texas)

Copano Bay with a battalion of infantry.

October 2: Texian victory at the battle of Gonzales. Centralists retreat to Béxar.

October 3: Mexican congress passes "Decree of Seven Laws" and frames a new constitution to replace the previous 1824 document.

October 9: Cós takes command of centralist army in Béxar. Total centralist strength is 647 *soldados*.

October 10: Texians capture Presido la Bahía at Goliad.

October 11: Stephen Austin takes command of the "Army of the People."

October 28: Texian victory at battle of Concepción.

November 1: Texians besiege Mexicans in Béxar.

November 24: Austin turns command over to Colonel Edward Burleson.

December 5–9: Battle of Béxar.

December 11: "Army of the People" accepts centralists' surrender.

December 12: Centralist army under General Cós surrenders San Antonio de Béxar to the Texians and retreats to Monclova, Mexico.

December 20: Third Texas Declaration of Independence proclaimed at Goliad.

December 30: Mexican Minister of War Tornel passes the Tornel Decree. "All foreigners who may land in any port of the [Mexican] republic or who enter it armed and for the purpose of attacking our territory shall be treated as pirates."

1836 **January 17:** Houston arrives in Goliad to prevent a Texian invasion of the Mexican port of Matamoros. James Grant has taken over command of the Texian army. Houston meets Bowie there, and orders him to Béxar to destroy the Alamo. Houston marches with Grant's army to Refugio.

General of Division Martín Perfecto de Cós. Allegedly a relative of Santa Anna, he invaded the province of Texas in the fall of 1835, marched overland and reinforced the garrison at Béxar. By the first week of December he had lost Béxar and what seemed the entire region. After surrendering honorably and being paroled never to bear arms against Texas again, he returned to Texas with Santa Anna in the late winter. He was captured two days after the San Jacinto battle. (Benson Latin American Collection, University of Texas at Austin)

February 2: James Walker Fannin lands at Copano with 200 U.S. volunteers.

February 3: Travis arrives in Béxar with about 30 cavalrymen, mostly regulars.

February 4–5: Fannin marches his small command to Refugio to join the Matamoros Expedition.

February 7: Fannin learns of the centralist invasion.

February 8/9: David Crockett arrives in Béxar as a private soldier in Harrison's Company of Tennessee Mounted Volunteers.

February 10–23: Houston treats with Cherokee Chief Bowles.

February 11: Alamo Commander J.C. Neill leaves and turns temporary command over to Travis.

February 12: Alamo garrison elects Bowie as commander, usurping Travis. Fannin retreats to Goliad. Reorganizes command at Presidio la Bahía, now renamed Fort Defiance.

February 16: Santa Anna crosses Río Grande.

February 17: General José Cosme de Urrea crosses Río Grande at Matamoros.

February 18–19: Reports reach Béxar that the centralists are crossing the Río Grande.

February 23: Centralists arrive and capture Béxar. Travis alerts colonies.

February 24: Bowie succumbs to his illness and turns command over to Travis.

February 25: Centralists attack the south wall of the Alamo. Texians respond by burning the *jacales* outside the walls. Captain Juan Seguín leaves the garrison as a courier. Travis's initial message reaches Fort Defiance.

February 27: Urrea kills or captures Johnson's command at San Patricio.

February 29: Ceasefire at the Alamo for three days. Most *Tejanos* leave the Alamo with Bowie's blessing.

March 1: "32 Men from Gonzales" arrive at the Alamo at 1:00 AM.

March 2: Texas independence declared at Washington-on-the-Brazos. Urrea kills or captures Grant's remaining Matamoros detachment at Agua Dulce Creek.

March 3: Bonham returns to the Alamo with good news of reinforcements from the colonies. Three more Mexican battalions arrive in Béxar. Centralists establish the Northern Battery and will move it closer to the Alamo each evening.

March 4: Santa Anna holds a council of war to discuss the assault on the Alamo.

March 5: *Soldados* move into their attack positions around the Alamo.

March 6: Final Alamo battle occurs from 5:00 to 6:30 AM.

March 8: The first Lone Star flag of Texas is raised over Fort Defiance.

March 11: Houston arrives in Gonzales to take command—again. Fannin orders Captain Amon B. King to Refugio to evacuate colonists. General Ramírez y Sesma departs Béxar for San Felipe de Austin and Colonel Morales for Goliad.

March 12: Fannin receives order from Houston to march to relieve the Alamo. King has meeting engagement with Centralist *Tejano* Cavalry, in reconnaissance for Urrea's main body.

March 13: Fannin prepares to march when King requests reinforcements at Refugio. Fannin dispatches the Georgia Battalion, who march 24 miles (39 km) in 12 hours. Susannah Dickenson arrives by escort at Gonzales. Houston fires the town and retreats.

March 14: Urrea arrives in Refugio with 1,500 *soldados*. The Georgians escape, but King's men are captured.

March 16: King's men are executed in compliance with the Tornel Decree. General Tolsa leaves Béxar to join General Ramírez y Sesma.

March 17: Houston's federalist army arrives at Burnham's Ferry on the Colorado River. The Texas Constitution is ratified by the delegates. Fannin learns of Refugio defeat.

March 19: Fannin retreats to Victoria. Houston destroys Burnham's Ferry and retreats to Beason's Crossing.

March 19–20: Battle of the Coleto. Fannin surrenders and command is marched back to la Bahía.

March 21: General of Brigade Ramírez y Sesma arrives opposite Beason's Crossing. Due to flooding he cannot ford. Santa Anna leaves Béxar

Going Visiting, c. 1853, by Friedrich Richard Petri. Though painted nearly 20 years after the war, this image accurately depicts family life in the Texian colonies. (Center for American History, the University of Texas at Austin)

to join with Ramírez y Sesma.

March 23: Houston learns of Fannin's surrender.

March 24: General Gaona departs Béxar for Mina en route to Nacogdoches.

March 26: Houston retreats to San Felipe de Austin.

March 27: Fannin's men are executed at Goliad.

March 28: Houston arrives at San Felipe.

March 29: Houston orders Mosely Baker to burn San Felipe and retreats to Groce's Plantation on the Brazos.

April 1: Secretary of War Rusk leaves Harrisburg to join Houston and relieve him of command.

April 11: The "Twin Sisters" cannon arrive for Houston's army.

April 12: Houston retreats from Groce's Plantation.

April 20: Texian and Mexican forces both arrive at San Jacinto. There is a small skirmish in the late afternoon.

April 21: Battle of San Jacinto.

April 22: Santa Anna is captured. Orders withdrawal of all Mexican forces from Texas.

April 26: Mexican Army begins retreat to Río Grande.

May 14: Treaties of Velasco are signed.

June 15: Mexican army retreats across the Río Grande at Matamoros.

Mexican revolutions

"All foreigners, who in virtue of the general law of 1824 which guarantees the security of their persons and property in the territory of the Mexican Nation, wish to remove to any of the settlements of the state of Coahuila y Texas are at liberty to do so; and the said State invites and calls them."

Article 1, Mexican Law, 1824

Mexico was a place of death. It came in many forms: from disease, or Comanche Indians, or revolution. At the beginning of the 19th century Mexico emerged from Spain's colonial system of *encomienda*, or rather ethnic exploitation. It was a system bent on exporting the minimum number of Spaniards to work the land, utilizing the enforced labor of the indigenous people, and then delivering the raw materials back to Spain. It spawned an environment that would lead to invasions and numerous revolutions, including the Texian War of Independence.

Spain's attempt at colonizing the northern province of Tejas had failed. There were only three settlements, Nacogdoches, San Antonio, and Goliad, containing a total population of around 2,500 *Tejano* prior to 1820. The solution was to bring in colonists from the United States. New England Yankee Moses Austin began negotiating with New Spain's governor in San Antonio de Béxar to establish Anglo-Saxon colonies in Tejas as a way of escaping his debts. When he presented before the authorities, Tejas was then an administrative division of the Viceroyalty of New Spain, or the Eastern Interior Provinces. The other provinces were Nuevo Leon, Coahuila and Nuevo Santander (later Tamalipas). With the assistance of an old acquaintance, Baron de Bastrop, Governor Antonio María Martínez forwarded the colonization request to General Joaquín

de Arredondo, who ruled the viceroyalty for the Crown. Arredondo approved the petition on January 17, 1821. En route to his home in Herculaneum, Missouri, Austin contracted pneumonia and died. On his deathbed he asked that his son, Stephen, "prosecute the enterprise he had commenced."

In the meantime, General Agustín de Iturbide with his "Army of Three Guarantees" marched into Mexico City on September 27, 1821, precipitating another revolution. Iturbide proclaimed Mexican independence under a new constitutional monarchy, with himself at the head. Spain rejected the Treaty of Cordoba (signed quickly with local Crown authorities) and although the Crown did not formally recognize Mexican independence until December 28, 1836 with the Treaty of Madrid, Mexico threw off many of the restrictive colonial practices imposed by Spain.

Two Iturbide commissioners from San Antonio, Juan de Veramendi and Erasmo Seguín, met Stephen Fuller Austin upon his arrival in Natchitoches to claim his father's grant. Austin was instructed in the conditions for Anglo colonization: colonists must be of good background, law-abiding, and must become Catholics. Austin agreed and on February 18, 1823 an imperial decree approved Austin's request.

Iturbide ruled Mexico as Emperor Agustín I until federalist forces led by Santa Anna overthrew him in March 1823. The new Constitution of 1824 joined the various former Spanish districts into states forming a union. The constitution was liberal and modeled after that of the United States. In the new republic, Texas did not receive statehood (as she had had under Spain); instead Texas became a territory of the state of Coahuila, and the southern border became the Río Nueces instead of the Río Grande.

A Map of the British Empire in America, with the French and Spanish Settlements, 1733. This map shows how the settlement of North America came to be split between those of Anglo and Iberian descent. (Texas State Library and Archives Commission)

Under the terms of the new republic, Texan statehood would be forthcoming once the population reached a certain number.

Mexico negotiated with more *empresarios* and the population on the land between the Río Colorado and Río Brazos increased. North American settlers were lured by the prospect of cheap, fertile land, and by 1831 the settler and slave population of Texas was 20,000, far outnumbering the Mexicans. In just ten years Stephen F. Austin, through skill and determination, had accomplished what over

a century of Spanish colonization attempts had failed to do. With this rapid population growth came a perceived danger to the Mexican authorities. The Anglos brought their own ways, including the belief that the rights they had held under the U.S. constitution, were God-given and were just as applicable in Mexico. Largely Protestant, few could speak much Spanish and they felt no loyalty to the Mexican state. Austin described the Mexican character, "*Dios castga el escandalo mas que el crimen*" ("God punishes the exposure more than the crime."); unlike the less flamboyant Mexicans, the Texian colonists did everything with as much exposure and posturing as possible, arousing the disapproval and dismay of the Mexican authorities.

The outbreak of hostilities

In 1828 Mexican President Guadalupe Victoria ordered General Manuel de Mier y Terán to Nacogdoches to assist with a border survey. He stated in his report that there were "...colonists of another people, more aggressive and better informed than the Mexican inhabitants, but also more shrewd and unruly; among these foreigners are fugitives from justice, honest laborers, vagabonds and criminals...The incoming stream of new settlers was unceasing; and the first news of them came by discovering them on land which they had already long occupied; the old inhabitants would then set up a claim of doubtful validity."

The following year, while serving as Commanding General of the Eastern Interior Provinces, Terán made several recommendations to the presidential usurper, Anastacio Bustamente. He suggested positioning troops on the Río Nueces, reinforcing the existing garrisons, increasing fortifications along the U.S. entry corridor (the Sabine River), and the recruitment of European and Mexican colonists. This report was modified by Bustamente as the "April 6 Law," which included Article IX, "The introduction of foreigners [meaning immigrants from the United States] across the northern frontier is prohibited under any pretext whatsoever... " Though Terán had not recommended so drastic a measure, with that decree, legal colonization by settlers from the north halted.

Terán stationed Col. José de las Piedras at Nacogdoches commanding 350 *soldados*; Col. Juan Davis Bradburn, with his 150 *soldados*, was ordered to build a customs house at Anahuac; Col. Domingo de Ugartechea was to build fortifications at Velasco; Lt. Col. Francisco Ruiz to do likewise at Tenoxtitlan on the Río Brazos; Capt. Enrique Villareal at Lipantitlan on the Río Nueces; Col. Pedro Ellis Bean was to occupy Fort Terán on the Río Neches; and finally former boundary commissioner Rafael Chovell was to garrison the Río Lavaca. Many of the *soldados* under

General Manuel de Mier y Terán. A scientist as well as an army officer, Terán drafted a report in 1828 that led to the creation of the April 6 Law, which stopped legal Anglo-American colonization into Texas. (Benson Latin American Collection, University of Texas at Austin)

Bradburn were convicts, working to earn their freedom and then be placed as seed for future Mexican growth in Texas. Convict soldiers did not fit with Anglo-Celtic sensibilities and any disturbance within the colonies was blamed on these prisoners. Nevertheless, the colonists were surrounded.

In 1829 Spain had invaded Mexico in one final attempt to keep their foothold in North America. The man who rose to defeat the Spaniards at the battle of Tampico would control the destiny of Mexico for two generations, leading the country to the brink of ruin, rescuing her, then destroying her again. He had learned his profession from Arredondo at the Río Medina in 1813 and under his tutelage, he had learned how to manage insurrection—especially Anglo-Celtic-led insurrection. His name was Antonio López de Santa Anna Perez de Lebron.

The "hero of Tampico" was neither centralist nor federalist, but both, sometimes concurrently. He had no devotion to any

Agustín I, c. 1822. The first emperor of Mexico, Agustín Iturbide represented a taste of what was to come with centralist Mexican politics. (Museo Nacional de Historia, Mexico)

cause other than the winning one. In 1830 Vice-President Anastacio Bustamente overthrew the legitimate government and declared for centralism. Santa Anna refused any position within the new regime and was hailed as a federalist of principle. The colonists in Texas were watching and regarded him as a kindred spirit.

Later that same year, Mexico abolished slavery. Not surprisingly, this resolution was unpopular in Texas, where the settlers regarded slaves as private property and no business of the government.

With the April 6 Law, all legal immigration from the U.S. had stopped. All *empresario* contracts were nullified, costing countless colonists and investors their life savings and cramping the economics of the colonies. Other than two small Irish colonies at San Patricio and Refugio, Mexicans and Europeans were unwilling to move to Texas, regardless of government subsidies. Without immigration to increase the population, the colonists would never achieve statehood.

Taxes, duties and slave emancipation became the law. To the American colonists

The Battle of Tampico, 1829 by Charles Paris. This painting is probably the most valuable image in the study of the Mexican Army's material culture during the Texian War of Independence. Though it is dated 1829, the painting was completed sometime in the 1830s, just prior to the war. General Santa Anna is shown in the left center, wearing a green undress frockcoat with blue sash (identifying him as a General of Division) and chapeau with tri-colored plumes. The frock coat is interesting because Travis' slave, Joe, recalled Santa Anna after the Alamo as being plainly dressed "…like a Methodist preacher…" Could this have been the uniform he wore at the Alamo? Behind him are his general staff, and behind them a *jacales*, a structure similar to those around the outer walls of the Alamo. In the right foreground are *grenaderos* and at least one dragoon (with black and pewter helmet and in buff/yellow coat). The flaming grenade on their shakos and cartridge boxes identifies the *grenaderos*. The *soldado* in the red is no doubt a "music" who wears the same coatee of his assigned unit, but with the colors reversed. Note he is also applying basic lifesaving skills to the wounded *granadero*. Behind him is a *soldado* wearing the fatigue hat. On the left and behind the general staff is a mounted unit wearing busbies or colpaks. It is interesting that Santa Anna chose to have himself surrounded by only the elite units of the Mexican Army. Sadly missing (and no doubt those who did the most fighting and dying) are the *fusileros*. (Museo Nacional de Historia, Mexico)

accustomed to a large degree of self-determination, these new laws seemed like unnecessary interventions on the part of a government that wanted to punish them and restrict their actions.

Two Anglos were placed in charge of duty enforcement, George Fisher and John Davis Bradburn. Both men were unpopular and were believed to be more loyal to the Mexicans than to their own people, especially Bradburn, who held a colonelcy in the Mexican army. Bradburn ordered all ships to bring in their cargos at his post, despite the lack of facilities, which put craft and crews at risk. The colonists ignored him. The inability to enforce this simple rule would make all customs laws untenable, so Bradburn declared martial law, used slave labor and confiscated private property. Finally, in the spring of 1832, he arrested two hotheads, William Barret Travis and Patrick C. Jack, attorneys at law, and placed them in a brick kiln. Travis and Jack were radical members of the War Party, keen to separate Texas from Mexico by any means possible. The Mexican authorities, not surprisingly, took exception to their protests and, in particular, Travis's provocative rumor-mongering, and incarcerated them.

The Texians, who could stand no more, responded by marching 200 militiamen to Anahuac, captured Bradburn's entire cavalry force of 19 *soldados* and held them for exchange. One hundred sixty men laid siege to the tiny compound. At one point, Bradburn staked the two lawyers spread-eagled to the ground with muskets pointed at their heads, ordering the colonists to withdraw. Travis was ready for this high-drama and yelled to his compatriots to attack anyway.

Following a day-long skirmish, the colonists agreed to parlay, retired to nearby Turtle Bayou and released the cavalrymen. Travis's martyrdom would have to wait. Bradburn still refused to repatriate his prisoners, and the colonists again skirmished with his forces, before withdrawing to Turtle Bayou to await artillery. The colonists, who were delivering this artillery from Brazoria, were stopped en route by the *soldados* of Col. Domingo de Ugartechea at Velasco. A battle ensued and the Mexicans surrendered.

That year the *grito* had sounded again in Mexico. Santa Anna's plan was simple—reinstate the federalist constitution of 1824 and restore an elective congress to the republic and the states. Santa Anna had little trouble in seizing control. It appeared that the Mexican republic would be federalist again.

While they waited for their artillery, the small army raised against Bradburn drafted the "Turtle Bayou Resolutions," which declared for the insurrectionist Santa Anna, for the Constitution of 1824, and for Texas to be a part of Mexico. As the Santanistas gained power, including some of Bradburn's superiors, Bradburn released his hostages and the Mexican garrison was removed to the Río Grande. The colonies would be federalist once more. Better representation, jury trial and restoration of immigration and statehood were yet to be achieved.

The colonists organized a convention in October 1832. Separate Mexican statehood was their only agenda. Rather than take their affairs to far-off Saltillo, the state capital of Coahuila, with no real representation, they desired what their forefathers had created for them—the ability to control their own destiny. Their mistake was in perceiving the Mexican federalists as fellow republicans. The convention asked that the April 6 Law be repealed, for a three-year exemption from customs duties and for statehood within the Mexican republic. The resolution was forwarded to the *ayuntamiento* (town council) in Béxar. It went no further. A second convention was called in 1833. A new colonist became chairman to draft a state constitution. He was a lawyer, a Jacksonian (he had fought with U.S. president Andrew Jackson in 1814) and former Democratic governor of Tennessee—Sam Houston. The convention nominated Stephen Austin to carry the convention's proposals to Mexico City.

It took Austin three months to reach Mexico City, and he arrived on July 18, 1833. This was not his first visit and he understood the Mexican temperament probably better than any Anglo in the region. Through countless appointments and lobbying, Austin got the April 6 Law repealed. The authorities granted various other concessions, except statehood, which was flatly refused. Austin started home.

Upon arrival in Saltillo, he was arrested for insurrection. While in Mexico City, he had written a letter advising the *ayuntamiento* of Béxar to plan for statehood. The Mexicans regarded this letter as a *grito* and *pronunciemento* (announcement of intent), always the first two steps in any respectable revolution. Austin was sent back to Mexico City and imprisoned for treason. The "Father of Texas" would not be repatriated until July 1835. Upon his return to Texas, this man who had counseled peace, moderation and compromise, denounced Santa Anna as "a base, unprincipled bloody monster," and announced that "War is our only recourse. No halfway measures, but war in full."

In April of 1834, Santa Anna having purposely let fail several liberal reforms, changed ideologies again. He ousted his federalist vice-president, dissolved the republican congress and state legislatures, called for the confiscation of weapons and dismissed all cabinet ministers. Revolts broke out, most severely in Coahuila and Zacatecas. His relative, General of Division Martín Perfecto de Cós, would mop up in Coahuila. Santa Anna looked to Zacatecas. On May 11, 1835, 2,500 Zacatecans were slaughtered. This would serve as his message to all who opposed him. The Texian colonists watched in silence.

On September 21 Texas was invaded. Cós and his column landed at Copano Bay near Goliad and began moving inland toward Goliad and Béxar. Finally, in October, the Mexican Constitution of 1824 was abolished.

The "Army of the People" faces the "Napoleon of the West"

The Leaders

Stephen Fuller Austin (1793–1836) was born in Virginia and grew up in southeastern Missouri. Upon the death of his father, Moses, he kept alive his father's dream of Anglo colonization of Mexico. More than any other colonist, Austin considered himself a loyal Mexican and tried to convince other Texians to emulate his belief. He was placed in jail in 1833 for inciting rebellion, an event that angered his fellow colonists and unwittingly served as a catalyst to the growing war party. Upon his release, he assumed the mantle of leadership and took command of the "Army of the People," leading it after the initial victory at Gonzales and marching to Béxar. He soon left his command to raise funds in the United States. He ran for president of the new republic in the fall of 1836 but was defeated by Houston and served as his secretary of state. Still ill from his time in prison, Austin died prematurely on December 27, 1836.

David Gouverneur Burnet (1788–1870) was 48 during the war and was the interim president of the Republic of Texas. He became an early advocate of secession from Coahuila and home-rule. His eight-month tenure as president was a series of peaks and valleys...mostly valleys. He often angered his cabinet, Vice-President Zavala and Houston, although he risked his own life to ensure

Lorenzo de Zavala was a native of the Yucatán and had already spent time in prison for his federalist sentiments. He served as a Mexican congressman and helped draft the Constitution of 1824. During the 1830s he became an *empresario* in Texas and was later governor of the Mexican state of Mexico. When Santa Anna usurped the presidency, he fled into Texas and became *ad interim* vice-president of the republic. He died shortly after the war in November 1836 and is buried in his family's cemetery on the San Jacinto battlefield. (Center for American History, the University of Texas at Austin)

that Santa Anna was not lynched after the revolution. He became vice-president in 1841, was Secretary of State for the Republic of Texas, and later a U.S. senator after annexation. He stood against Texas secession from the United States and lost his only son to the Confederate cause.

Sam Houston (1793–1863) was the same age as Austin. At 16, he had left his home in Tennessee and lived with the Cherokee until war began with Great Britain. He served in the ranks of the U.S. regular army during the War of 1812 and was promoted to lieutenant after his bravery during the battle of Horseshoe Bend, where he was seriously wounded—a wound that would cause him pain the rest of his life. He became governor of Tennessee and was publicly embarrassed by a scandal when his bride of three months left him. He resigned from office in 1829 and returned to the Cherokee. He arrived in Texas in 1832. He played little part in the 1835 campaign but

was named commander-in-chief in March of 1836. After the revolution he became the first president of the Republic of Texas in the fall of 1836 and went on to serve in the U.S. senate.

Lorenzo de Zavala (1789–1836) was a native of Yucatán who had fled to Texas during the centralist usurpation; he was the only elder statesman of Texas. He was in his late 40s

Stephen F. Austin, by William Howard c. 1833. The "Father of Texas" was painted in Mexico City prior to his arrest and imprisonment. Austin is wearing a black hunting frock with a shot bag made of ocelot or jaguar fur, and sports a rifle nearly as tall as himself. This is the last image of Austin in good health and of peaceful countenance. His visit was a failure and his imprisonment turned him from a dove into a hawk. (Center for American History, the University of Texas at Austin)

during the revolution and had previously served as governor of the state of Mexico, and in the Mexican senate. During the War of Texian Independence he was the interim vice-president of Texas and lived at the confluence of Buffalo Bayou and the Río San Jacinto, just across from the battlefield. He caught pneumonia and died in the fall of 1836.

Attorney and one time schoolteacher, William Barret Travis (1809–36) had been a vociferous voice for the war party since at least 1832. He immigrated to Texas after leaving his wife and two children in Alabama, though he later gained custody of his son, Charles. He was of Scottish descent, read Sir Walter Scott and was so taken with his Celtic tribal forebears that he even addressed his military superiors as "chieftains." A talented lawyer, his self-confidence and brusque manner often made him appear arrogant, although his leadership skills at least caused his men to respect, if not like, him.

James Bowie (1796–1836) was a long-time resident of the "old southwest." Having traded in real estate, mustangs and slaves, he married into minor Mexican aristocracy and secured larger land holdings for himself. He was shattered by the death of his wife and children from cholera in 1833 and took solace in heavy drinking, although it is unclear exactly what incapacitated him at the Alamo. He commanded the colonists at their victory at Concepción in December 1835 and was ordered by Houston to destroy the Alamo and deliver the armaments to the interior of Texas. He disagreed with this order and co-signed a letter with James Neill stating "we would rather die in these ditches, than give it up to the enemy." And he did.

James Walker Fannin (1804–36) was a 32-year-old Georgian. Illegitimate, he had attended the United States Military Academy from 1819 to 1821 under his grandfather's name. Later, he made amends with his natural father and assumed his name. He arrived at Velasco in 1834 and joined the growing war party. He was with Bowie at Concepción and commanded the Texian garrison at Goliad where he was executed on Palm Sunday, 1836.

The Texians, mainly frontiersmen, were faced by the regular army and reserve soldiers of Mexico, led by the charismatic Antonio López de Santa Anna de Perez de Lebron (1794–1876). Intelligent, handsome and occasionally generous, he was also vain, ruthless and unprincipled. Aged 42 in 1836 and president-general of Mexico, he reveled in his nickname, "Napoleon of the West." His abdication of the republican presidency and cancellation of the 1824 federalist constitution, as well as the closure of the state legislatures ignited the Texian War. He ordered executions of prisoners at Zacatecas, the Alamo, San Patricio, Refugio, Goliad and Guadalupe Victoria. These, more than any other events, caused his eventual defeat by large numbers of motivated volunteers from the U.S. intent on avenging their former countrymen. It is impossible to define Mexico in the 19th century without understanding him.

Major General Vicente Filisola (1789–1850) was 47 and served as second-in-command of the Army of the North. Italian by birth, he was raised in Spain and immigrated to the viceroyalty of New Spain in 1811. He served in a variety of royalist and later Mexican military positions, even becoming a minor *empresario* in east Texas. After the surrender, he assumed command of the Mexican army in Texas and signed the Treaty of Velasco before retreating into Mexico. For this action he was tried, although he exonerated himself in 1841.

Major General Manuel Fernandez y Castrillón had served with Santa Anna since at least 1822. He was a veteran of numerous campaigns and was well respected by his peers and subordinates. He assumed command of one of the assault columns at the Alamo and was in tactical command at San Jacinto where he was killed. His body was located by his friend, de Zavala, and buried in his small family cemetery near the Texian encampment.

Major General Martín Perfecto de Cós (1800–54) was 36 during the war and allegedly a relative of Santa Anna. He arrived in Texas in the fall of 1835 after he had closed the legislature of Coahuila y Texas, and took command of the province, establishing his headquarters in Béxar. He was driven from the region in the winter of 1835, but returned with the invading army in the 1836 campaign where he commanded a column during the assault on the Alamo. He was captured two days after the battle of San Jacinto and was soon repatriated to Mexico.

José Cosme de Urrea (1797–1849) was the 39-year-old commander of the centralists' eastern column attacking up the coastal road. He was the most aggressive and skilled of all the Mexican commanders. It is doubtful that the battle of San Jacinto would have taken place if he had been in command that day. He disagreed with Filisola on the retreat to Mexico. Upon his return to Mexico, he remained involved in the dual Mexican role of military officer and political agitator.

The armies

For many American settlers, Texas provided a second chance. Most of the leaders and many of the volunteers were failures in their past lives, and Texas took away the sting of that failure and the opportunity to overcome their past.

Texas had been placed under the Republic of Mexico's Militia Act of 1822, which organized three militia districts—at Nacogdoches, La Bahía and San Antonio. The district judge commanded two cavalry battalions and one of infantry. They had their own uniform and flags, and were organized around the population bases. This structure was modified and expanded as the colonists moved into the fertile area between the Brazos and Colorado Rivers. Militias were maintained to guard against the ever-present threat of servile insurrection or Comanche incursions. From 1834, Béxar, Brazos and Nacogdoches were the three administrative districts of Texas. Colonists were sorted into organized and unorganized militias.

In November 1835 the consultation created an army consisting of regulars, existing organized and unorganized militia and a

Colonel José Cosme de Urrea commanded the Mexican column that invaded along the coastal road into the Texian colonies. He defeated the Texians at the battles of Refugio and Coleto and was arguably the best of the Mexican commanders. After the surrender when Filisola offered the command to a native Mexican, Urrea did not volunteer, but later criticized his colleague's decisions. (Benson Latin American Collection, University of Texas at Austin)

Volunteer Auxiliary Corps (VAC). This provided structure and leadership to the federalist Army of the People then besieging Béxar. Houston was named as overall commander of the Texas Military Forces, which consisted of the organized militia (units that were already in existence), and a regular force organized after the United States Army model that would consist of one brigade of 1,120 soldiers. The brigade would have one regiment of artillery and one of infantry. Furthermore, each regiment was organized with two subordinate battalions (one commanded by a lieutenant-colonel and the other by a major) with a company strength of 56 soldiers. In December a legion

Equestrian Portrait of General Santa Anna, engraved
by W. H. Dodd [n.d.]. Hand-tinted engraving,

(Prints and Photographs Collection, University of
Texas at Austin)

of cavalry was added. The VAC was to be manned by volunteers from the United States.

Despite the initial good intentions, the regular army never formed more than one company (which fought under Millard at San Jacinto), although there were also some cavalry and artillery, heavily augmented by deserters from the 3rd United States Infantry (regulars from Louisiana, a 19th-century form of covert aid, from General Gaines at Fort Jessup). U.S. Regulars or not, these troops would be better categorized under the VAC, rather than as the Texian "regulars." Some of the officers, like Travis of the Legion of Cavalry, bore so-called regular commissions and had small numbers of men under the regular structure. The overwhelming majority of soldiers who fought came under the categories of existing militia, such as the "Gonzales Mounted Ranging Company of Volunteers" or into the VAC, such as the numerous units at Goliad or San Jacinto, which arrived in the early winter or spring of 1836. Even the colonists recognized the need for organization of what Governor Smith

referred to as a "mob called an army." The war did not last long enough for such big plans to take effect. The volunteers did, however, provide the nucleus for the Army of the Republic of Texas, which was formed after the victory at San Jacinto.

The Mexican Army went through many modifications following independence. Major reorganizations occurred in 1821–22, 1823 and again in 1833, and the Mexicans borrowed heavily from the Spaniards. The army was organized around the regular forces called *permanentes* and the organized militia, the *activos*. Army officials organized the infantry into battalions and cavalry into regiments. The unorganized militia (which, at least in principle, governed the colonists as well) consisted of every male aged from 18 to 40 who could bear arms.

Corrida de la Sandia (Watermelon Race), c. 1890, by Theodore Gentilz. Though this print postdates the war by decades, the supporting research and sketch were no doubt completed when Gentilz visited Texas in 1844. The game was comparable to rugby on horseback—with fewer rules. (Daughters of the Republic of Texas Library at the Alamo)

The ten battalions consisted of eight companies, six *fusilero* and the two preferred companies of *cazadores* (riflemen—literally "hunters") and *granaderos*. There were the usual command and staff, and a small detachment of pioneers. Each *permanente* battalion was named for a hero of the many Mexican wars of independence—Matamoros, Allende, Aldama, Jimenez, etc. The *activo* battalions had the same organization, but were named for their hometown or province.

There were only six regiments, with four squadrons apiece. Each squadron consisted of two companies. The regiments were named for battles of the revolution, such as Dolores or Tampico. The cavalry wore red tunics faced green and crested goatskin helmets with silver furniture. The infantry uniform consisted of a blue coatee with red facings and brass buttons. Trousers were blue, gray or white, and the shako sported brass furniture, a national cockade and pom-pom. Musicians of both branches wore identical uniforms that had the colors reversed. Their Texian opponents had no uniform and wore their own clothing.

The *presidiales,* the remaining mounted Mexican force, had no real comparison with any other units in the west: they acted as policemen, soldiers and security for the mission framework. They had been created to deal with the mounted southern plains Indians who harassed the missions and still existed in 1836, organized in 32 companies throughout northern Mexico. In Coahuila y Texas, there were nine *permanente presidial* companies and another two in *activo* status.

"Come and take it"

"The Anglo-American spirit appears in everything we do; quick, intelligent, and comprehensive; and while such men are fighting for their rights, they may possibly be overpowered by numbers, but if whipped, they won't stay whipped."

David B. MaComb, Gonzales veteran

The colonists had named the town of Gonzales, the capital of the DeWitt colony, for Governor Rafael Gonzales of Coahuila y Texas, to show their appreciation and loyalty to the republican government. In 1831 Mexico presented the town with a 6-pdr. (2 kg) cannon for local defense against the Indians.

The colony was pro-government and was not a seat of unrest in the same way as San Felipe or Anahuac. In September 1835, a *soldado* assaulted the town sheriff, Jesse McCoy, with his musket. With the militia disarmament order of the President-General and the arrival of Cós, tensions were high and the pro-government climate of Gonzales changed. Shortly afterward, Col. Domingo Ugartechea ordered the return of the cannon. The community refused.

Lieutenant Francisco Castañeda and his Alamo Presidial Company arrived on September 29 across the Río Guadalupe from Gonzales to reinforce de Ugartechea. The boats were secured on the colonists' side of the river and the Gonzales Ranging Company of Mounted Volunteers prevented the *presidiales* from fording. Castañeda bivouacked 300 yards (274 m) from the fording site and waited. The Texians sent to the other colonies for more volunteers.

Dr. Lancelot Smither, a Gonzales colonist, was in Béxar when he discovered the situation. He volunteered his services as an intermediary to Ugartecha and left for his home, accompanied by three *soldados*. When he arrived at the Mexican bivouac he explained his role to Castañeda, who welcomed the assistance. Smither carried the message of goodwill to the Texian pickets, although this was not relayed to their militia commanders.

On October 1, Castañeda marched seven miles upriver where he could ford safely. The Texians had determined to not wait on an attack and, moved by the spirit of Lexington and Concord, (when American colonists attacked British troops during the American Revolution) began to cross the river to attack the centralists. The Texians numbered less than 200 militia, and the Béxar Presidial Company around 100 *soldados*.

The morning of October 2 was overcast and foggy. The Texians were forming on the farm of Ezekiel Williams and breakfasted on some of his watermelons. At 6:00 AM the Texians began skirmishing with the *presidiales*. Castañeda responded with a cavalry charge and the Texian line retreated. Inside the Mexican lines, Castañeda arrested Smither and confiscated his property. As the fog lifted and full battle became more likely, he paroled Smither to parlay with his fellow colonists. Once inside the Texian lines, the militia commander arrested him as a spy. Smither convinced the colonel to meet with Castañeda and the two walked into the middle of the lines for parlay. Castañeda stated that he was only there to request the cannon, not to seize it, and that he too, was a federalist. The Texian commander told him that he was on the wrong side and should join them in the revolt against centralism. Castañeda responded that he was a soldier and obliged to obey orders. The parlay ended and both returned to their lines.

The Texian flag, the first to bear a Lone Star, was made by two local women. It was white with a cannon and star, and the words "Come and take it!" in black. (The motto

Veramendi House, the home of James Bowie prior to the battle of the Alamo. Texian Ben Milam was killed in front of this building during the battle of Béxar. All that remains today are the front doors, located in the Alamo Shrine. (Daughters of the Republic of Texas Library at the Alamo)

was reminiscent of Leonidas, King of Sparta's response to Darius at Thermopylae: when asked to surrender his arms, he replied "*Molen Labe,*" or "Come and get them").

Lt. Col. James Neill fired the disputed cannon and the Texian line erupted in musketry as well. The Texians did not advance and Castañeda, his duty complete and not wanting to start a revolution, ordered a retreat to Béxar.

The Texian War of Independence had begun.

Following this "victory," around 500 colonial militia and volunteers mustered in Gonzales. Austin accepted command of the "Army of the People" and regimental officers were elected. Their goal was the Mexican garrison under Ugartechea at Béxar, and reinstatement of the Constitution. On October 9, Cós arrived in Béxar, bringing

the total centralist strength to around 751 *fusileros* and *presidiales.*

Unbeknown to the colonists gathering in Gonzales, Capt. George Collingsworth and his Matagorda Militia attacked and seized the *presidio* La Bahía, capturing 30 or so *soldados* who had been left behind as Cós advanced toward Béxar. The Texians had not only won their first engagement, but had also taken their first fortification.

The centralists prepared Béxar for battle. The first major engagement occurred at Mission Concepción, two miles (3 km) south of Béxar. The colonists, under the joint-command of James Bowie and James Fannin, assumed a defensive position in an elbow of the Río San Antonio. The centralists attacked, were beaten and retreated into Béxar with 120 casualties. They prepared for a siege, while the colonists consolidated around Béxar and waited.

In November, William Travis was conducting reconnaissance operations along the Río Atascosita. He discovered a *remuda* of 300 centralist horses. He attacked and drove off the *soldado* patrols and captured the horses.

He then led the herd 70 miles (113 km) north to the colonists' lines. This was a minor nuisance for the centralists, but the third major victory for the colonists. The Texians soon lost respect for the *soldados'* abilities.

In November, with a centralist force bottled up in Béxar, Austin stepped down as commander and a General Council convened in San Felipe, the nominal Anglo capital of Texas, to discuss the formation of a provisional government. Winter approached and discontent and boredom spread among the colonists around Béxar. They left, going home to their stores and farms with VAC newcomers fresh from the U.S. replacing them. The number of Texians capped at around 300 men by the end of November.

A group of Texian officers decided to retreat to Gonzales. On December 4 the men were in ranks, ready to march east. Ben Milam, an impresario and former republican soldier, was tired of the vacillation and rode up to the formation yelling, "Who will go with old Ben Milam into San Antonio?" 200 men returned the shout and formed up to fight.

The battle of Béxar began at 3:00 AM the next morning and lasted for five days. It was a bitter house-to-house fight with both sides suffering high casualties. In front of the Veramendi House, just off Main Plaza, a Baker rifle bullet killed Ben Milam. He was the first of many Texian martyrs.

Cós surrendered on December 10. His men were placed on parole; they could keep

Map of the battle of Béxar. After the battle of Concepción, the Texians closed in on Béxar. They marshaled at the Old Mill north of town and attacked in two battalions into Béxar, which soon caused the surrender of the centralists.

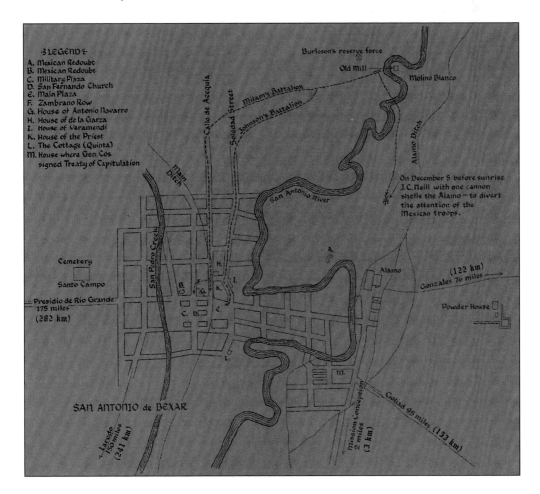

Church of Mission Nuestra Señora de la Purisima Concepción. It was here that the four companies commanded by Fannin and Bowie defeated the centralist forces of Cós. (Texas State Library and Archives Commission)

their weapons and one cannon and were allowed to march out of Béxar with full military honors. They agreed never to take up arms against the Texians again. Three months into the war, the Texians had won six battles and all centralist forces had been ousted from their country.

Idle time is no friend to the soldier. During the winter months several schemes arose. The most notorious was to take the federalist revolution to the Mexican border, where it would surely spread. Houston (now commander of all forces in Texas, or at least those who paid him attention) partially stemmed the tide of those Matamoros-bound adventurers at Presidio la Bahía—renamed Fort Defiance. There were over 400 Texian volunteers commanded by the hero of Concepción, Col. James W. Fannin. In Béxar, most of the volunteers had already left for Mexico with most of the provisions, leaving only 100 or so men (and 20 of these were wounded from the previous battle) under Col. James C. Neill.

Houston requested permission of Governor Smith to order the Alamo demilitarized and all stores and cannon evacuated to the colonies. He sent Bowie ahead to Béxar to prepare for the eventuality. Smith disagreed and ordered that the Alamo be defended. At about this time Houston took a furlough and went to treat with the Cherokee. He did not return to the colonies until March 1836.

El Camino Reale

Santa Anna organized his army of the north at San Luis Potosi, dividing his forces into two columns. The main effort, under Santa Anna himself, marched north and west through the former capital of Saltillo, then across the Río Grande at Presidio del Río Grande. He followed the course of the old Spanish road, *El Camino Reale*, defended by San Antonio de Béxar and the Alamo. The second force, commanded by General of Brigade (Acting) José Cosme de Urrea, marched due north along the coast and across the Río Grande at Matamoros, sweeping up the coastal road toward the interior of the colonies. The total for the invasion was 6,000 *soldados*.

It was an enveloping movement and the armies were capable of destroying anything caught in between the two forces. Cós, from Laredo, joined Santa Anna's column. The *soldados* (many accompanied by their families) marched through unforgiving desert and unseasonable blizzards, the worst in a century. Any who expired were left behind without being buried. The casualty rate of that march surely equaled that of the battles to come.

Santa Anna brought more than an army. He brought legislation. On December 30, his Secretary of War had passed into law articles dealing with insurrection. Every colonist found to have taken part would be executed. Every foreigner taken under arms would be considered a pirate and executed. Santa Anna had absorbed these important lessons serving as a youth with Arredondo, and had perfected them the previous spring on his own people.

On February 2 both Bowie and Neill concurred with Governor Smith that the Alamo should be held. Bowie and Neill wrote to Houston, "…we would rather die in these ditches than give it up to the enemy." Fortunately, the centralists under Cós and the presidial cavalry before him had fortified the former mission.

The same day as the Bowie–Neill missive, Lt. Col. William B. Travis arrived with 30 regular cavalrymen in Béxar, and agreed with the other two that the Alamo was "…the key to Texas." On February 8 Neill took leave and turned command over to Travis. That same day former U.S. Congressman David Crockett arrived as a private in the company of Harrison's Tennessee Mounted Volunteers. That brought the Texians in the Alamo to around 140 defenders, with 10 to 12 being *Tejanos*, and possibly one free black.

West Side, Main Plaza, San Antonio, Texas, 1849 by W.G.M. Samuel. Behind the San Fernando Church is a flagpole in Military Plaza, where the Texians raised their rebellious Twin-Star flag of Coahuila and Texas as the centralists entered Béxar on February 23, 1836. (Courtesy of Béxar County and the Witte Museum, San Antonio, Texas)

The 1836 Campaign

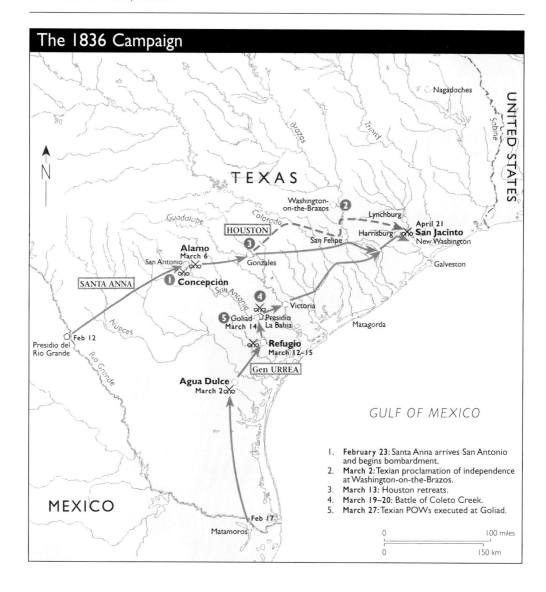

UNITED STATES

Nagadoches

TEXAS

Washington-on-the-Brazos ❷

Lynchburg

Guadalupe

Colorado

HOUSTON ❸

San Felipe

Harrisburg

April 21
San Jacinto
New Washington

Alamo
March 6

San Antonio

Gonzales

Galveston

SANTA ANNA

❶ **Concepción**

San Antonio

❹

Victoria

❺ Goliad Presidio
March 14 La Bahía

Matagorda

Feb 12
Presidio del
Rio Grande

Nueces

Rio Grande

Refugio
March 12–15

Gen URREA

Agua Dulce
March 2

GULF OF MEXICO

1. **February 23:** Santa Anna arrives San Antonio
    and begins bombardment.
2. **March 2:** Texian proclamation of independence
    at Washington-on-the-Brazos.
3. **March 13:** Houston retreats.
4. **March 19–20:** Battle of Coleto Creek.
5. **March 27:** Texian POWs executed at Goliad.

MEXICO

Feb 17

Matamoros

0   100 miles

0   150 km

Travis's assumption of command created problems. He held a regular commission, yet Bowie provided the volunteers. On February 14 they agreed to co-command. The Alamo compound was strengthened and more volunteers moved in from their quarters in Béxar.

The Texians did not believe the centralists would march before spring, and although there were reports to the contrary, there was no real effort to prepare for hostilities. The 40 or so cavalry in the fort conducted neither organized reconnaissance nor screening. Most of the livestock was grazing on the neighboring *rancheros*.

The Texians needed little excuse to celebrate. On February 22 a *fandango* occurred in honor of George Washington. Sometime after midnight a courier arrived and warned the Béxareños that there was centralist cavalry on the Río Leon, eight miles (13 km) away. No one informed the Texians.

Fortunately for the Alamo garrison, the heavy rains had kept the 290 cavalrymen of the advance guard under General of Brigade Joaquin Ramírez y Sesma from crossing the swollen Río Medina. Santa Anna's plan to surprise the Texians in their bunks had failed. The attack would have to be in the morning.

"Victory or Death"

The Texians' defense line was along the San Antonio River where it intersected the El Camino Reale (at the Alamo) and the coastal roads (Fort Defiance). The Texians occupied these fortifications along the colonial frontier intending to delay the centralist forces who must march up these two roads. Once the Mexicans arrived in either area, the colonists would reinforce the garrisons. On February 16 Santa Anna crossed the Río Grande at Presidio del Río Grande, and the following day Urrea crossed at Matamoros.

Early on February 23, following the *fandango* to celebrate Washington's birthday, the inhabitants of San Antonio de Béxar (800 yards west of the Alamo) awoke to the sound of *carreta*—wheels squeaking and oxen lowing—as the majority of San Antonio's

North Side, Main Plaza, San Antonio, Texas, 1849, by W.G.M. Samuel, showing the Yturri House, Santa Anna's headquarters during the Alamo siege and battle. (Béxar County and the Witte Museum, San Antonio, Texas)

citizens left town. There had been a rumor the night before that the army of Santa Anna was bivouacked on the Río León, eight miles (13 km) away, and could attack at any time.

Travis started detaining citizens, demanding to know their destination. Their answers were simple—out of Béxar. Doubtless many of them recalled the last Anglo-participated insurrection in 1813, when the royalist army executed Béxareños alongside the filibusters. Those who had managed to avoid the firing squad often had their property confiscated.

Travis posted a sentry in the tower of the San Fernando church on Main Plaza with an eye toward the west; he suspected that Santa Anna would attack from the direction of the Laredo or the Upper Presidial roads. Just after noon, the bell rang and the sentry called, "the enemy are in view!" Travis dispatched John Sutherland and John Smith to reconnoiter. Just over the Alazan Heights,

North Side Main Plaza San Antonio TEXAS 1849

west of town, the two came upon the Dolores Cavalry Regiment (Reinforced), preparing to attack the town. Upon their return to Béxar at the gallop, Travis ordered a full retreat into the Alamo.

Defending the Alamo

As the Alamo gate closed behind the Texians (now numbering about 150 men, as well as a dozen non-combatants), the advance guard of the vanguard brigade entered Béxar. Three companies of *cazadores*, three of *granaderos*, the cavalry and two 7 in. (17.8 cm) howitzers captured San Antonio. The remainder of the vanguard bypassed San Antonio to ensure there were no federalists two miles (3 km) away at the Mission Concepción. The Mexicans raised a blood-red banner over the San Fernando church, indicating that no quarter would be shown to the Texians. The

18-pdr. (8-kg), the heaviest cannon in the Alamo, fired in response. There would be no quarter for the Mexicans either. Soon the Texians dispatched two separate couriers asking for parley. Each time the Texians received the same response: surrender at discretion or be put to the sword.

Over the next few days, each side attempted to organize the situation. On February 24 the Mexicans erected at least one battery and conducted pre-combat inspections of their preferred (*cazadore* and *granadero*) companies. The Texians' well was insufficient for the garrison. This would lead

San Fernando church as it appears today, although a church has been on the same site since 1795. The Texian sentry was in the left tower (there was no right tower in 1836) and spotted the advance guard of the centralists on February 23. Later that day, Santa Anna hoisted his red flag of no quarter from the same bell tower. (Library of Congress, Prints and Photographs Division HABS, TEX,15-SANT,9-3)

Lt. Col. William Barret Travis, commandant of the Alamo. He was an outspoken agitator and made a name for himself with the Mexican government in 1832. His famous letter from the Alamo begs "Victory or Death," while his last, nine days later, only asks to be remembered to his son. (DeGolyer Library, Southern Methodist University, Dallas, Texas)

to several skirmishes over control of the *acequia* (water source) over the next several days. That evening, the Texians sent out patrols and captured a *soldado* who they used to help interpret the Mexican movements. Bowie's illness became acute and he turned full command over to Travis. His first act was to compose one of the more stirring pieces of American military literature, an appeal to his countrymen for support, which noted that despite the fact that the fort had "sustained a continual Bombardment and cannonade for

24 hours…our flag still waves proudly from the walls—I shall never surrender or retreat. Then, I call on you in the name of Liberty, of patriotism and everything dear to the American character, to come to our aid… if this call is neglected, I am determined to sustain myself as long as possible and die like a soldier who never forgets what is due to his honor and that of his country. Victory or Death." They were stark and emotive words, but they appeared to fall on deaf ears.

Both forces were confident but cautious and by February 25 the siege could have gone either way. The Mexicans attacked first with the task-organized battalion of *cazadores* and the *permanente* Matamoros Battalion.

The attack position was in the vicinity of the river, probably between the river battery and the ford. The assault was personally

commanded by General Fernandez y
Castrillón with Santa Anna in the area. The
column forded the river and attacked up
through the *jacales* (huts constructed from
mesquite poles) and outbuildings of Pueblo de
Valero, apparently getting as close as 50 to 100
yards (46 to 91 km) from the Alamo walls.

The *soldados* were driven back from the
pueblo into La Villita after about two hours,
suffering light casualties. This engagement
was not a victory for the Texians as it
allowed the Mexicans to establish artillery
and infantry entrenchments in both La
Villita and the *alameda*.

During the fighting, and again in the
evening, the Texians dispatched men with
torches and fired those *jacales* closest to the
Alamo, clearing their fields of fire. Travis
mentioned Crockett in his report, as
"animating the men to their duty." That
evening Capt. Juan Seguín was sent to
Houston with another plea for assistance,
while Santa Anna ordered General Gaona and
his brigade to hurry on to San Antonio.

Alamo Battlefield Map, March 1836, by Colonel Ygnacio de
Labastida. Labastida was a Mexican staff engineer officer
during the Alamo siege and battle. Labastida gives us the
only known period map that provides the Alamo (slightly
enlarged) in context with the communities of Béxar, La
Villita and Pueblo del Alamo. This is considered the most
accurate siege rendering of the Alamo. (Barker American
History Center, the University of Texas at Austin)

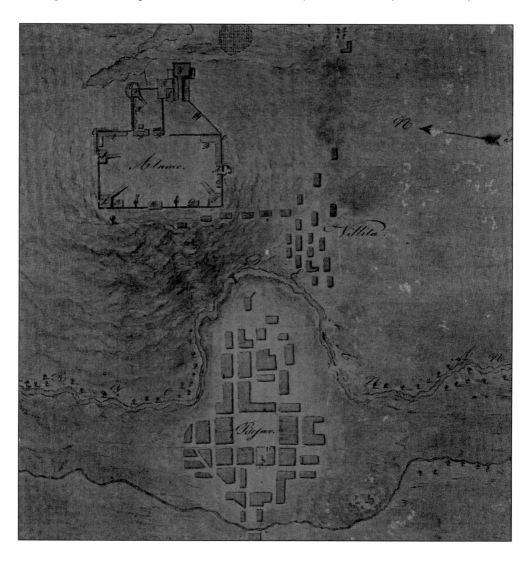

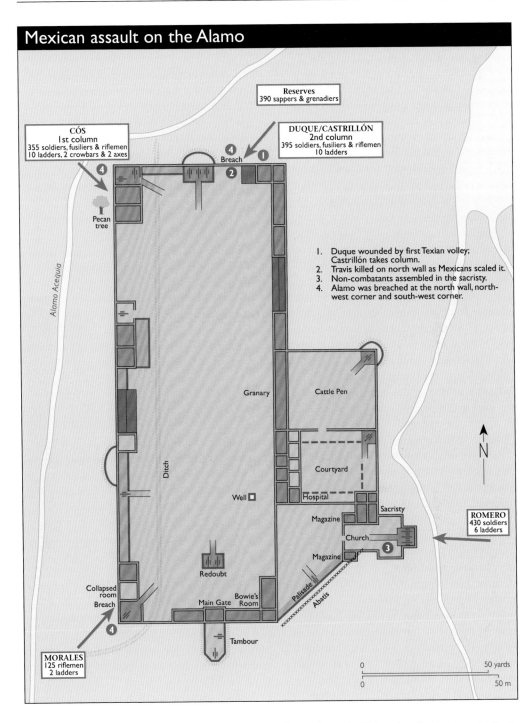

Mexican assault on the Alamo

Reserves
390 sappers & grenadiers

CÓS
1st column
355 soldiers, fusiliers & riflemen
10 ladders, 2 crowbars & 2 axes

DUQUE/CASTRILLÓN
2nd column
395 soldiers, fusiliers & riflemen
10 ladders

Breach

Pecan
tree

Alamo Acequia

1. Duque wounded by first Texian volley;
   Castrillón takes column.
2. Travis killed on north wall as Mexicans scaled it.
3. Non-combatants assembled in the sacristy.
4. Alamo was breached at the north wall, north-
   west corner and south-west corner.

Granary

Cattle Pen

Ditch

Courtyard

N

Well

Hospital

Sacristy

ROMERO
430 soldiers
6 ladders

Magazine

Church

Magazine

Redoubt

Collapsed
room

Breach

Main Gate

Bowie's
Room

Palisade

Abatis

MORALES
125 riflemen
2 ladders

Tambour

0   50 yards

0   50 m

Receiving Travis's initial message, Fannin ordered a relief march to the Alamo with 300 men and four cannon. Within 200 yards (183 m) of departure from Goliad, one of his wagons broke down. Once across the river a council of war was called and the officers "unanimously determined" to return to Fort Defiance to complete the fortifications.

The next day, February 26, a "norther" blew in. The garrison's water situation became more tenuous and precipitated a skirmish in the early hours near the *acequia*, east of the Alamo. The Texians were repulsed and a larger battle started. During the evening the Texians again tried to draw water from the *acequia*, but fire from the *cazadores'* Baker rifles prevented this.

The Mexican army also needed provisions, so on February 27 foraging parties were sent out to local *ranchos*. The Mexicans cut off the *acequia* at the Río San Antonio, forcing the Texians to survive on their limited well water. Gaona received Santa Anna's order and sent three battalions of his brigade to San Antonio.

The following day, the Mexicans gained intelligence that 200 Texian reinforcements were en route from Goliad. Santa Anna ordered an infantry battalion and the cavalry under General of Brigade Ramírez y Sesma to advance down the Goliad Road to attack the Texian reinforcements. He reminded Ramírez y Sesma that there would be no prisoners of war. On February 29 the Mexicans also proposed an armistice of three days and the Texians accepted it. The majority of *Tejanos* left during this ceasefire.

At 1:00 AM on March 1, 32 men of Gonzales Ranging Company of Mounted Volunteers reinforced the Alamo garrison. The forces of Ramírez y Sesma advanced toward Goliad some distance and then returned to Béxar. The Mexicans constructed more trenches. The Texians fired two 12-lb (5.4 kg) shells toward town, hitting the Yturri House, Santa Anna's headquarters. The armistice was finished.

Santa Anna dispatched more couriers to hurry along Gaona's Brigade.

At 11:00 AM on March 1 James Bonham entered the Alamo "unmolested" with news of more reinforcements. A letter from Travis's former law partner declared that 600 men were soon to be en route to Béxar. The Texians fired several cannon and muskets into the city.

Across the river, the Mexicans also received good news: Urrea's column had routed the Texians at San Patricio. The lead elements of Gaona's Brigade arrived in San Antonio bringing two infantry and one assault engineer battalions. All the Mexican artillery was moved to a battery 300 yards (274 m) from the Alamo's north wall.

Santa Anna called a council of war. He questioned whether they should wait for the arrival of the remainder of Gaona's Brigade (expected after March 7) before beginning the final assault. He reminded his commanders there would be no prisoners, which caused a rift among his subordinates. The council was adjourned with no resolution on the attack date. Later that night, one or two *Tejanas* from the Alamo informed the Mexicans of the defenders' status, expected reinforcements and possible surrender plans if no more Texians arrived.

This news decided Santa Anna, who ordered the final assault on March 5. The plan called for four assault, one reserve and one cavalry columns. The *soldados* bedded down at twilight. At midnight, all columns began to move toward their attack positions.

Once in their attack positions, the *soldados* laid down for some sleep. They had neither coats nor blankets, so the cold ground sucked all their body heat from them and it is doubtful that their sleep was restful. At 5:00 AM on March 6 a *soldado* from the second column could wait no longer and cried out, "Viva Santa Anna!" The other columns seconded this cry, and, surprise lost, Santa Anna ordered rockets fired and the massed battalion and regimental bands to blow the *degüello* [the Spanish tune of no quarter, which literally means, "to slit the throat"].

All four Mexican columns surged forward, and the Texians were awakened by the thunderous noise of hundreds of running feet and shouts for the Mexican Republic. It did not take the Texian gunners long to discharge their cannon into the noisy onrush. Those *soldados* in the front ranks paid a high price for their noisy patriotism.

The Alamo's enfilade fire from the eastern batteries forced the eastern column to shift north and join the northern columns in a confused mass at the base of the north wall, directly under the Texian cannon; but this position was useless in taking the fortification. Santa Anna ordered his reserve

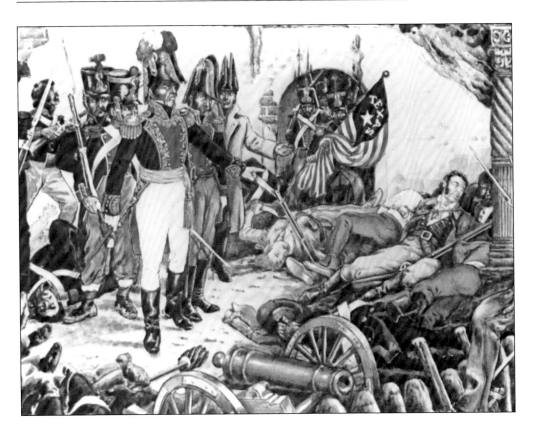

The Alamo, 8:00 AM by Joseph Hefter. Seen from just over the palisade where it intersects with the church, Crockett lies dead *prior* to Santa Anna's inspection. Crockett is dressed more like the former U.S. congressman he was than the backwoodsman character the public (then and today) would have preferred. In the small opening of the *convento*-connecting wall, a *soldado* emerges with the Lone Star and Stripe flag that may well have been at the Alamo. (DeGolyer Library, Southern Methodist University, Dallas, Texas)

column into the attack to regain the momentum. The reserves were past the mob and on top of the north wall in minutes. It must have been very soon thereafter that Travis, fighting from the north wall, was shot through the forehead and tumbled down the cannon ramp.

At the same moment, the lone southern column of *cazadore* breached the Alamo at the southwest corner. The Texians retreated into the adobe apartments, the *convento* and the church and poured a withering fire from their supplemental defensive positions, but it was short-lived. The *soldados* took the

Texians' un-spiked guns and turned them on their former masters, rolling the pieces up to the doorways and blasting them down. Once inside, the remainder did not take too long. Near the final phase of the battle, about 60 Texians left their positions and ran for the Gonzales Road—the road to the colonies and home. Awaiting them was the Mexican cavalry column, posted on the same road anticipating this situation. The lancers made quick work of the refugees.

By 6:30 AM, the battle was over. Several prisoners were executed and the non-combatants were taken into Béxar, where they were interviewed by Santa Anna and released. The survivors numbered about 16 and were mainly *Tejanos* and their children who had remained within the walls of the Alamo.

What happened next was almost biblical in its appearance. The bodies of the defenders were dragged outside the Alamo to the Alameda at the Gonzales Road. There, at least two pyres were built: a layer of Texians, then a layer of wood, no doubt with coal, oil and kindling added. The remains were then fired and the bodies were soon awash in the funerary flames. The location where this occurred was almost as important as the action itself. The Gonzales Road was the main road into the colonies and most, if not all of the defenders had arrived in Béxar on this road. Santa Anna may have been reminded of the Spartacan slave revolt in 70 BC which ended with the Romans crucifying the defeated along the Appian Way to warn all who dared to challenge Rome. With such public humiliation, Santa Anna must have hoped to accomplish the same fear in his very own client state.

The Mexican campaign continues

Santa Anna needed to marshal his forces before continuing on with the campaign. Over the next several days, his drawn-out column began arriving in Béxar. On March 8 Gaona arrived with the active battalions of Querétaro and Guanajuato and six guns. The next day General Filisola, second- in-command of the Army of the North, arrived. The last of the cavalry arrived on March 10.

As the units arrived Santa Anna worked on plans for the pursuit of the remaining forces and suppression of the political centers of Anglo-Texas. Urrea was marching up the coast road and would no doubt encounter Fannin's command within a fortnight. On March 11 Col. Morales marched with the Jiménez and San Luís Potosi battalions to reinforce Urrea. That same day, General Ramírez y Sesma marched for the Texian colonial capital, San Felipe de Austin, with the squadrons from Dolores, Veracruz and Tampico, as well as the Alamo-

In December 1854, Elizabeth Crockett, widow of David Crockett, received this certificate from the State of Texas, entitling her to the sum of $24 owed to her late husband for his service at the battle of the Alamo. (Texas State Archives and Library Commission)

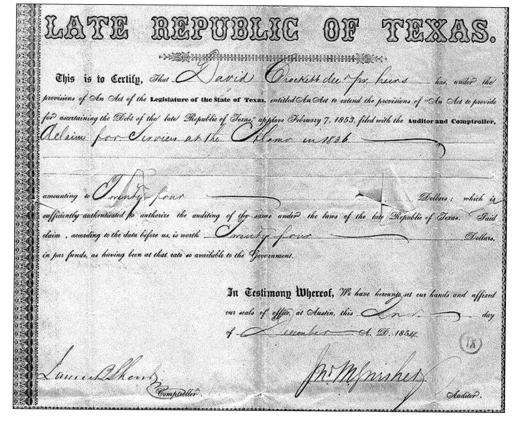

bloodied battalions of Aldama, Matamoros, and Toluca with two cannon. He was ordered to prevent the colonies from reinforcing their garrison at Goliad. He was followed in support, on March 16, by General Tolsa's brigade consisting of the 1st Active Battalion of Mexico City and the permanent battalion of Guererro. That same day, colonels Montoya and Bradburn marched the active

Crockett led before Santa Anna, by John W. Thomason, Jr. (1934). Here is an entirely different view of Crockett's final moments. He is brought as a prisoner before Santa Anna, bound and wounded, but still not defeated and he maintains his dignity. (DeGolyer Library, Southern Methodist University, Dallas, Texas)

battalions of Tres Villas and Querétaro to Copano, near Goliad. On March 24 General Gaona's brigade marched toward

Alamo Funeral Pyre, by Jose Cisneros (1979). One can barely make out the human forms bathed in the flames of one of two funerary pyres near the Alameda, on the Gonzales Road. The *soldado* leaning against a cottonwood, with a kerchief over his nose to filter out the fumes of burning flesh, is the most striking image in the drawing. Nearer to the pyre, two Béxareños also cover their faces to keep out the stench. Perched on a tree above the *soldado* are two turkey buzzards, waiting for the heat to die down. (DeGolyer Library, Southern Methodist University, Dallas, Texas)

Nacogdoches via Mina, with the Morelos and Guanajunto battalions, three cannon and 20 *presidiales*. Santa Anna followed Ramírez y Sesma's route to San Felipe de Austin on March 31 taking his escort of 30 dragoons and staff. He had split his forces into three, like sabers thrusting at the colonies: Gaona sweeping north had 700 *soldados*, Urrea in the south had over 1,300, and Ramírez y Sesma marched straight through the center with 1,400 troops. Aside from Fannin at Goliad, there was no organized force in Texas to stop him.

The National Convention at Washington Town

While the Alamo was under siege, the 59 delegates to the convention at Washington Town (later named Washington-on-the-Brazos) were running out of time. From November 1835 Texas was governed by a General Council composed of representatives from each municipality of the state. The Council called for a National Convention to organize a government, and elected delegates in February 1836. The town barely lived up to its title, or so wrote William Fairfax Gray: "About a dozen wretched cabins or shanties constitute the city; not one decent house in it, and only one well defined street. A rare place to hold a national convention in. They [the delegates] will have to leave it promptly to avoid starvation."

The delegates met on March 1 knowing that an army besieged their garrison at the Alamo and that another force was marching up the coastal road. Yet they remained. In an unfinished building, these men framed not only the declaration of independence, but a constitution as well. Texas would have laws before she had even earned her freedom.

George Campbell Childress, one of two delegates from Milam, arrived with a

Independence Hall, Washington Town. Much less than a hall, it was an unfinished gunsmith shop rented to the convention for $170. There were no windows or doors so cloth was placed over the openings to kill the draft. It was a humble beginning for the republic. (Special Collections Division, University of Texas at Arlington Library)

completed declaration and read it to the convention on March 2. The document mirrored the United States model, in that it outlined a series of grievances perpetuated by the Mexican dictatorship on the colonists of Texas. After signing the document on March 3, five copies were dispatched to key towns within the colonies. Childress further proposed the icon that represents Texas and Texans to this day, "a single star of five points."

On March 15 the delegates learned of the fall of the Alamo and the news caused "complete panic." A proposal was made to withdraw to safer environs, but cooler heads prevailed and the delegates chose to remain until their work was complete and Texas had a government. The convention lasted 17 days and eventually re-nominated Houston as commander-in-chief of all Texian military forces. On March 6 Houston left for Gonzales to raise and organize the army and march to the relief of the Alamo. Additionally David G. Burnet was appointed interim president of

The Reading of the Texas Declaration of Independence, by Charles and Fanny Normann (1936). George C. Childress, author of the declaration, reads it to the Texian delegates at Washington Town on March 2, 1836. It would be signed the following day. Sam Houston is seated in the left foreground, Lorenzo de Zavala on the right. (Joe Fultz Estate, Navasota, Texas, Blinn)

the republic, with Lorenzo de Zavala as the vice-president. Thomas Jefferson Rusk was named Secretary of War. De Zavala was from the Yucatán, but there were two native-born *Tejanos* (José Antonio Baldomero Navarro and José Francisco Ruíz) who signed the document. De Zavala had served as president of the committee to draft the original "Constitution of 1824." After the convention, he returned to Buffalo Bayou, his home. The Texians would later utilize his house as a hospital after the battle of San Jacinto.

The men who made up the convention were as diverse as their interests. They were from five foreign countries and 12 states of the U.S. Ten of the delegates were colonists prior to 1830, but 15 had arrived in the province the previous year. They were doctors, lawyers, mechanics, and businessmen—and even former state Supreme Court justices. Sam Houston, who attended as a delegate, had been defeated in his home district of Nacogdoches, and was at the convention representing tiny Refugio.

On March 17 the interim officers were sworn into office. The first cabinet meeting was held a few hours later and Thomas Rusk declared that they "were in a terrible condition and they ought to go take a drink, get on their horses, go to the army, and fight like hell till they got out of it."

The coastal road and Goliad

General Urrea marched north. His column consisted of 601 *soldados* of the Active Yucatán Battalion (reinforced) and the *permanente* Cavalry Regiments of Cuautla and Tampico, with a squadron from the Active Durango Regiment and one 4-pdr. (1.8 kg) cannon.

On February 27, reinforced with Tory *Tejano* and Karankawa Indian cavalry, Urrea attacked and routed the remainder of the abortive Matamoros Expedition under Johnson and Grant. All were killed, except for five or six who escaped. Some of the survivors made their way to Fort Defiance where they informed Fannin of the Mexican force's size and position.

Colonel James Walker Fannin Jr., by Samuel F.B. Morse. Fannin appears here, probably, in the uniform of the Georgia Militia, to which he belonged prior to immigrating to Texas. If the painting is Fannin, the steely look of determination surely must have been added as artistic license. (Bridgeman Art Library/Dallas Historical Society, Dallas, Texas)

The Irish Colony at the Mission (Refugio), 28 miles south of Goliad, asked for assistance in removing the colonists further to the north in anticipation of the Mexicans' arrival. Fannin ordered one company of the Georgia Battalion and all the garrisons' carts to assist with the move. The company arrived on March 12 and confronted Urrea's advance guard. Reinforcements were requested and the remainder of the Georgia

Battalion was marched to the colony, with orders to finish the task and quickly return to Fort Defiance. The next evening Houston ordered Fannin to destroy his fortifications and retreat east to the federalist-friendly town of Guadalupe Victoria. Since Fannin had dispatched all his wagons to Refugio, he ordered more carts brought up from Guadalupe Victoria.

Urrea ordered all his forces to mass at Refugio. The Georgians took refuge in the mission and nearby woods. During the two-day fight the Georgians managed an escape, under cover of a "norther," eastward to Victoria. Fannin sent courier after courier to determine the course of events, but all were captured, giving Urrea a solid picture of Fannin's situation. Fannin, with no cavalry, sat in his fort, unable to see even across the river.

On March 14 Albert C. Horton and 31 cavalrymen arrived with replacement carts from Guadalupe Victoria. Fort Defiance then contained 330 volunteers. Fannin still did not march for Victoria. On March 17 he received news of the Georgia Battalion's defeat at Refugio, which convinced him of the need to retreat.

Urrea had surrounded the Texian garrison with cavalry and centralist *rancheros*. No march would be made from the *presidio* without his knowledge. While Fannin's men prepared for retreat, the centralist cavalry was spotted. Fannin, who had ordered most of the cannon buried, ordered them dug up and remounted and prepared for a siege. He further ordered the town of La Bahia fired. The men were kept at their positions throughout the night of the 18th and morning of the 19th.

Convinced he would not be attacked, Fannin made up his mind and at around 9:00 AM the retreat started. It was a foggy morning and this no doubt concealed the Texian movements from the centralist cavalry who were observing the fort. Urrea did not learn of the march until two hours later. He galloped his cavalry in pursuit, followed by the infantry, now reinforced with two battalions fresh from Béxar. His artillery was readied for the march as well.

Since the Texians' oxen had been yoked all night in preparation for the march, they were hungry and uncooperative. Fannin ordered a halt halfway between Manahuilla and Coleto creeks, despite his officers' pleas for a later stop to take advantage of the protection of the wood line surrounding the Coleto River a mere two miles (3 km) away. Fannin disagreed. Horton's cavalry were posted to the front, but the rear-screen had failed, the men having fallen asleep. A cart broke down and more time was lost. At 1:30 PM, the Mexicans overtook Fannin.

The Texians responded with a skirmish line to protect access to the Coleto. They were 500 yards (457 m) from the creek when Fannin ordered his command to "Form square" and, with his artillery positioned at the corners, continued the march to the wood line. He must have remembered his successful defense of timber the previous December at Concepcíon. Another cart broke down. Urrea attacked.

The *cazadores* soon killed all the oxen, and the Mexican cavalry positioned themselves between the Texians and the creek. Urrea charged.

The Texians put up a sound defense. Centralist casualties were 50 killed and over twice that wounded. The three ranks of Texian infantry poured a devastating fire upon their attackers, but it was not enough. In their haste to retreat, they had not carried enough water and the wounded (including Fannin) and the men were soon dehydrated. The cannon would soon be useless without the water to swab the barrels after each shot. Night fell and the larger battle ceased, except for the *cazadores,* who kept up a fire on the Texians through the night, and Urrea's use of bugle calls to keep them off-guard. A "norther" blew in to add to their suffering.

Fannin called yet another war council and determined to fight one more day. They decided not to retreat under cover of night to the Coleto, for fear of abandoning the wounded. Barricades were fashioned from wagons, and trenches were dug the rest of the evening and early morning.

The remainder of Urrea's forces arrived on the battlefield and the centralists then numbered up to 1,000 *soldados*. He began his attack at 6:15 AM and within one or two rounds the Texians raised a white flag. Fannin requested conditional surrender, which Urrea refused, although he promised to forward their requests to the Supreme Government. Outnumbered, out of water, with no hope of succor from the colonies and outfought, Fannin unconditionally surrendered. The men were marched back to the *presidio* at La Bahia where the Georgia Battalion refugees, and a United States volunteer battalion captured as soon as they embarked from the boats at Copano, soon joined them.

Urrea did request clemency, which Santa Anna denied. Urrea and his command marched on to Guadalupe Victoria and left Col. Nicolas de la Portilla, with the Battalion of Tres Villas, in command of the *presidio*. Santa Anna ordered Portilla to execute the foreigners immediately. The next morning, Palm Sunday, March 27, the Texians were organized into three columns. They believed they were going home soon and several groups had been singing *Home, Sweet Home* the previous evening.

Each column took a different road from Goliad (La Bahia), either the San Antonio Road, the Victoria Road, or the San Patricio Road, with *soldados* marching in two ranks one either side of the Texians. After walking some distance from the *presidio*, the command was given to halt, and the single rank of *soldados* passed through their prisoners in order to form two ranks. Then the command was given to fire. Some Texians, realizing what was happening, kneeled in prayer, some begged for mercy and others returned the glares of their captors. The Texians reckoned that 342 men were murdered, although amazingly, about 30 men survived this massacre—the Mexicans left them for dead and some struggled to the nearby Río San Antonio.

Within earshot of the screams and musket shots, the wounded Texians were brought out of the tiny Loreto Chapel inside the *presidio*, most still in their bunks. Two *soldados* carried them out to the parade ground and sat them down. Then one of the *soldados* would lower his .75 musket at point blank to the prisoner's chest and fire. Fannin, wounded in the thigh and wearing a

Goliad Executions, by Norman Price. The Texians were marched out of the *presidio* in three separate columns, flanked on either side by *soldados*. Once each column arrived at its designated location, the *soldados* halted, and then passed through the Texians, forming two ranks on one side of their captives. They opened fire, then pursued the survivors with bayonet and lance. Over 300 Texians were killed in this manner. (Texas State Archives and Library Commission)

talma to keep out the damp, had to be helped outside. He was brought in front of the chapel and seated in a chair. He asked to speak to Portilla, but was refused. The officer commanding his firing squad said, through a translator: "For having come with an armed band to commit depredations and revolutionize Texas, the Mexican government is about to chastise you." Fannin was then shot in the head and face. His body stiffened and dropped from the chair and rolled into a tiny depression to his left.

The Texian army at Gonzales

Sam Houston arrived in Gonzales from the convention on March 11 with little or no army to command. Houston organized the 300-plus soldiers of the existing militia companies, mostly from Austin's Colony, into the 1st Regiment of Texas Volunteers, commanded by Kentuckian Sidney Sherman.

Juan Sequín, who could only provide ten-day-old information on the garrison at the Alamo, met Houston in Gonzales. On March 13 Susannah Dickenson, a non-combatant survivor from the Alamo, arrived in Gonzales with Travis's slave Joe and Santa Anna's servant Ben. She carried a letter from Santa Anna to Houston, declaring that the slaughter at the Alamo was an example of what would happen to the rest of Texas that remained in rebellion. Houston retreated that evening, burning Gonzales as he left. On March 17 he reached Burnham's Ferry on the Río Colorado; he burned it as well and continued in retreat. Two days later he arrived at Beason's Crossing where his army began to take shape.

Volunteers from the U.S. and eastern and coastal colonies began arriving, and Houston used the time to train his mob. On March 21 the column of Ramírez y Sesma arrived across the rain-swollen Colorado River from the Texian camp. Ramírez y Sesma dug in his limited Mexican artillery and waited for the river to subside. Houston did not push the *soldados* into a fight. Two days later he learned of Fannin's capitulation at Goliad. On March 26 Houston retreated to the

Brazos, putting one more river between his forces and the centralists. On March 28 he ordered San Felipe burned and continued his retreat to Groce's Plantation, the largest slave-holding estate in Texas. A retreating army is never in love with their commander and Houston's forces dropped to 500. While at Groce's, Houston organized the 2nd Texas Infantry Volunteers and transferred Sidney Sherman from the 1st Regiment as colonel. He also organized a four-company battalion consisting of the embryonic Texas Regulars. On April 11 two matched iron 6-pdrs. (2.7 kg) arrived in the Texian bivouac, a gift from the citizens of Cincinnati nicknamed the "Twin Sisters." With artillery, approximately

Juan N. Seguín, c. 1832, by Thomas Jefferson Wright, portrayed here as a soldier of the Texas Republic. (Texas State Library and Archives Commission)

60 cavalrymen and nearly 1,000 infantry, the Texas army was becoming a combined arms force.

The Texian Republican Army remained at Groce's until April 12. The steamboat *Yellowstone* took two days hauling the men across the river. The time spent had allowed Houston to train his soldiers and allowed for more volunteers to arrive from the U.S., including deserter U.S. regulars from Fort Jessup in Louisiana. Houston added this "clandestine aid" to the Regular Battalion and his artillery, and sprinkled the remainder in amongst the 1st and 2nd regiments.

Houston continued his march east, away from the enemy. His men distrusted him and his seniors disliked and trusted him even less. Would they march to the coast and fight the centralists, or retreat into the United States? On April 17 the army took

the last road to Harrisburg and the coast. The die was cast.

With the burning of Gonzales and San Felipe, and the twin disasters of the Alamo and Goliad, the colonists of Texas panicked. Most of these people had no desire to fight anyone and wanted only to protect hearth and home. They fled toward the Río Sabine and the United States border.

Santa Anna shadowed Houston's army and passed through San Felipe on April 9. He mounted 50 *cazadores* and *granaderos* on horses and took off after him, leaving Ramírez y Sesma with the remainder of the column. He could find no place to ford or cross the Colorado River, until, at Thompson's Pass, he captured a flatboat and two canoes from a rear-guard of Texians. Ramírez y Sesma rejoined Santa Anna on the 13th. Detaining local colonists, Santa Anna discovered the Texas government was then at the town of Harrisburg. Santa Anna decided to end the revolution with one bold move and accomplish what the British had failed to do three generations before—capture the government leaders in one swift stroke.

On the 14th he marched for Harrisburg with his preferred mounted companies, the battalion of Matamoros, his escort, and one cannon. He ordered the remainder of his army to muster at Old Fort. He would assemble all his columns, destroy the insurrectionist leaders, and defeat Houston in a bloody victory. He arrived in Harrisburg the next evening and burned it. From Harrisburg the government had fled to New Washington on the coast. Santa Anna paused, sending Almonte ahead to stop them. He had just missed the government, who had left at noon for a steamship for Galveston Island. A Frenchman told him that Houston was then near the pass at Lynchburg with 800 men and two cannon. He ordered Cós and 500 *soldados* to join him as soon as possible and left with his 700 *soldados* to march from New Washington to Lynchburg to meet Houston.

On April 20 Santa Anna's reconnaissance discovered Houston's arrival at Lynchburg.

At the same time, the Texians had discovered him. Sidney Sherman

(commander of the 2nd Regiment and no fan of Houston) was out conducting reconnaissance with 40 cavalrymen. At 1:00 PM Sherman rode up to the Texian camp on the banks of Buffalo Bayou in a stand of Live Oaks. Soon enough Santa Anna decided to force the Texians into battle. He advanced his cavalry and *cazadores* toward the Texians. The president-general ordered his musicians to play the *degüello*, which had brought him good fortune at the Alamo.

The "Golden Standard," the Mexicans' only cannon—a bronze 12 pdr. (5.4 kg)— was advanced to the center of the field and positioned in a copse of trees, protected by some *soldados* who opened fire at the Texians. They overshot the Texians, the cannon ball splashing harmlessly into Buffalo Bayou. The next round wounded Lt. Col. Neill, former Alamo commander. He was evacuated to the de Zavala house and took no more part in the battle.

The "Twin Sisters" answered the "Golden Standard." Santa Anna had arrived in the woods to observe the battle, and then returned to his planned campsite. Soon after, he ordered the *cazadore* company to return as well. The "Golden Standard" was unsecured.

Texians watching from the treetops of their bivouac called out this news to Houston. Sherman asked permission to capture the cannon; Houston refused. Angrily, Sherman attacked with 61 cavalrymen joined by Secretary Rusk. The Mexicans had almost withdrawn the gun to the crest of the hill in front of their camp. Santa Anna met the Texians with 50 dragoons and his *cazadores*. The withdrawal had been a ruse to tempt the Texians into attack, and it had worked. The dragoons charged the Texians, who had dismounted to re-load. The Texians fired and retreated back to their camp. Sherman had requested infantry support, but Houston refused it. Two companies of infantry finally arrived, but only to cover the cavalry's retreat. When all his forces were back on the banks of Buffalo Bayou, Houston admonished Sherman. A boat arrived and the men supped on fresh bread and coffee—their first in three days.

Santa Anna had his *soldados* sleep at their positions, awaiting reinforcements. He would not be safe until they arrived.

San Jacinto

The plain of San Jacinto (pronounced "ha-ceento") was hardly the flat coastal prairie so often imagined. The battlefield was bordered on the east by the San Jacinto River, to the south by Peggy Lake and in the north by Buffalo Bayou. There were two main roads into the battlefield, the Harrisburg–Lynchburg Road (which the Texians had marched in on) on the north and the New Washington Road on the west. The entire area, other than the roads, was surrounded with impenetrable marshes and morasses.

At dawn Santa Anna ordered the construction of breastworks composed of packsaddles, sacks of hard bread, and baggage. They extended from the marsh on their right to the Washington Road on their left, with a small gap in the center for the "Golden Standard." Lt. Col. Pedro Francisco Delgado, the president-general's staff secretary, expressed his dislike of the position to Gen. Castrillón, who replied, "What can I do my friend? I know it well, but cannot help it. You know that nothing avails against the caprice, arbitrary will, and ignorance of that man."

At 9:00 AM, Gen. Cós arrived with 500 *soldados*, and marched right past the Texians' right flank on the Washington Road. The addition of Mexican reinforcements was not lost on Deaf Smith, who was observing with some of the Texians. Smith said to no one in particular, "They have traveled our track. The bridge at Vince's ought to be burnt down. I will see the general." Smith went to Houston and asked permission to destroy Vince's Bridge to prevent more reinforcements. Houston asked, "Can you do it without being cut to pieces by the Mexican cavalry?" Smith replied, "Give me six men and I will try." Houston gave his permission and an admonition: "You will be speedy if you return in time for the scenes that are to be

The legendary scout Erastus "Deaf" Smith. He captured the critical bag of dispatches that showed that Santa Anna had split from his main force, and it was this information that prompted Houston to attack the Mexicans at San Jacinto before they could be reinforced. (Texas State Library and Archives Commission)

enacted here." Smith left at once with six men to destroy the bridge.

At noon Houston held a war council, his only one, and asked the question, "Shall we attack the enemy in position or receive their attack in ours?" There were several opinions offered, but the majority favored attack upon the Mexican works. Houston listened and proposed to build a bridge across Buffalo Bayou to the Texian rear, for further retreat. His officers did not agree and Houston declared, "Fight, and be damned."

At 3:30 PM Deaf Smith and his volunteers had succeeded in destroying the bridge. He rode into the Texian camp shouting, "Fight for your lives, Vince's Bridge is down."

At 4:00 PM Houston ordered parade and the Texian Republican Army formed in battle line. From left to right, 2nd Regiment (Sherman), 1st Regiment (Burleson), Artillery

The battle of San Jacinto

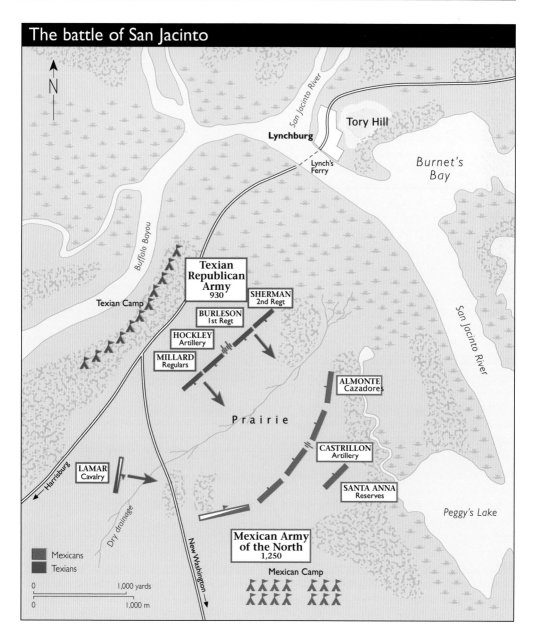

N

San Jacinto River

Tory Hill

Lynchburg

Lynch's Ferry

Burnet's Bay

Buffalo Bayou

Texian Republican Army
930

SHERMAN
2nd Regt

Texian Camp

BURLESON
1st Regt

San Jacinto River

HOCKLEY
Artillery

MILLARD
Regulars

ALMONTE
Cazadores

P r a i r i e

CASTRILLON
Artillery

Harrisburg

LAMAR
Cavalry

SANTA ANNA
Reserves

Peggy's Lake

Dry drainage

New Washington

Mexican Army of the North
1,250

Mexican Camp

Mexicans
Texians

0   1,000 yards
0   1,000 m

(Hockley), Regulars (Millard) and Cavalry (Lamar). "Accordingly at the above stated time the drum beat general parade [in] which [there] was cheering by every man," recorded one eye-witness. From this position, the command was given, "By the right of companies, to the front. Companies, by the right flank, right face. Trail arms. Forward." The Texian Republican Army was deployed in line with companies in column, an interesting maneuver that Houston probably used to keep his units aligned. Marching like this, they had only to follow the company commander and first sergeant of each company. The musicians, variously described as fifers, drummers, or a single black drummer, to fiddle players, played *Come to the Bower* and *The Girl I Left Behind Me*.

Halfway to the Mexican works, and using a natural depression, Houston deployed his forces into battle line, "By companies into line, march." The companies wheeled into

battalion formation across the army and continued their advance through the depression and up the slope in front of the Mexican line.

At 4:30 PM Sherman's 2nd Regiment, on the Texian left and attacking into a heavy wood line, opened the ball by making contact with the three *cazadore* companies on the Mexican right, commanded by Almonte. A *cazadore* bugler alarmed the remainder of the Mexican force. The rest of the *soldados* had stacked arms and the cavalrymen were dismounted and riding their horses bareback to water. Having been either in forced march or awake at their posts all night long, panic ensued in the exhausted Mexican Army.

As soon as the Texians gained the flat at about 300 yards (274 m) from the Mexican breastworks, the Mexicans opened artillery fire with the "Golden Standard." The Texians went to the Double Quick march, with arms at Right Shoulder Shift, to quickly close the distance. The "Twin Sisters" halted at 200 yards (183 m) and returned fire on the Mexican line. Santa Anna ordered the Guerrero Permanent Battalion to assault the "Twin Sisters," but the column was repulsed. At 60 yards (55 m), Houston rode in front of the Texian line, then dashed back through the

The Battle of San Jacinto, by Henry Arthur McArdle, (1895). McArdle thoroughly researched his topic, and though many anachronisms remain, this represents the most detailed picture of the genre. It shows the Texian's 1st Regiment as it hits the Mexican barricade. The Mexicans wear cotton fatigues, while their officers attempt to regain command and control. Houston is seen near the left center having lost his first mount, waving his men on toward the Mexican camp. In the right background, Santa Anna is fleeing on a borrowed horse. (Texas State Library and Archives Commission)

1st Regiment, yelling his concern that no more Mexicans arrive to help Santa Anna, "Not a man reinforcement! Not a man reinforcement!" Houston was wounded in the ankle (possibly by Texian gunfire) by the same volley that killed his white horse, Saracen. The Texians quickly freed Houston from the pinned horse and he was remounted. When the remainder of the Texian line was 40 yards (37 m) from the Mexican works, the Texians halted, fired, and charged.

The Texians kept firing as they advanced. The "Golden Standard" only fired three times before it was captured. Gen. Fernandez y Castrillón, already wounded in the leg, tried to keep the gun firing, but his gunners were shot down as soon as they were replaced, and his men began to run. He physically tried to stop them, then finally shamed them by climbing on the ammunition box, folding his arms, and proclaiming, "I have been in forty battles and never showed my back; I am too old to do it now." He stood there for a moment while the battle surged past him, seemingly ignored by the Texians advancing past him. Then he stepped down off the box and began walking after his panicked *soldados*. After a few paces, he again turned to face the Texians and was immediately shot down.

Santa Anna watched his command disintegrate: first on his right with the *cazadores*, his chosen men, flying past him crying, "It's no use, it's no use, there are a 1,000 Americans in the woods." He responded by first running from one position to the other wringing his hands and ordering *soldados* to take cover from the "Twin Sisters'" fire. Then he ordered a drummer to beat assembly, but the drummer replied that he could not because he was wounded; Santa Anna then called out to a bugler to blow the same. The second musician responded likewise. At that instant, a ball from one of the "Twin Sisters" decapitated a *soldado* standing near the president-general. Santa Anna exclaimed, "Damn these Americans, I believe they will shoot us all!" As his horse was unavailable, he was given the mount of his aide-de-camp, Col. José Batres, by the colonel's manservant. He mounted the solid black horse and sought out his personal escort. Finding only two still remained and that these were attempting to saddle amidst the chaos, Santa Anna left them and commenced his flight. Batres would not need the horse much longer; he would soon be killed in the swamp, bogged in the mud.

The panic continued unabated. It took only 18 minutes, once the battle was joined, to overrun the Mexican camp. The Texians were in as much disarray as the *soldados*. Houston was still concerned about the arrival of more Mexican reinforcements and knew that his Texians would just as easily turn this almost-victory into a rout. He attempted to halt the advance and regain command and control. "There has been glory enough for one day," Houston

declared. Rusk who was near him replied, "No it is not enough, while the enemy is in sight. General Houston, I have been your friend, but I have followed you long enough. The victory is not yet complete, the army shall go ahead." Then yelling to Sherman's men, "If we stop, we are cut to pieces. Don't stop—go ahead, give them hell."

And the Texians did just that, spurred on by a combination of disgust for a despised enemy, vengeance for the Alamo and the Goliad executions, and the carnage and summary executions. The slaughter occurred from the Mexican camp all down to the marsh bordering Peggy Lake. Almonte was seen swimming across Peggy Lake, to the southwest shore, holding his sword out of the water. At least one *soldadera* [female combatant] was not spared the bloodbath, nor were children who performed roles as musicians. Texian officers tried to halt the wanton slaughter, but to no avail. It was ghastly and one soldier when ordered to halt, replied, "If Jesus Christ were to come down and tell me to stop killing yellowbellies, I would refuse." Again, trying to halt the carnage, Houston declared, "Gentlemen, gentlemen, gentlemen. I applaud your bravery, but damn your manners."

Somewhere near dusk, after the bloodlust had cooled, Houston was able to finally parade his Texians and ordered them back to their camp across the field. As he rode through the former Mexican camp he saw Almonte marching 250 *soldados* to surrender, but Houston believed it was Cós with reinforcements (Houston did not know it was Cós who had arrived that morning. Cós himself would not be captured until April 23). Houston cried out, "Halt, that the fate of Texas now depends on the cast of a die, and that General Cós is coming up with reinforcements. All is lost, all is lost; my God, all is lost." A Texian soldier standing nearby handed him a spyglass from the camp debris and said, "Take this general, it will assist you in ascertaining what that is out there in the prairie." Houston glassed the approaching column and saw that it was a column of prisoners, controlled by Rusk.

Sam Houston, photographed by Mathew Brady's studio in the 1850s. (Library of Congress, Prints and Photographs Division LC-USZ62-110029)

The moment being too much for him, Houston broke down and cried out, "Have I a friend in the world? Colonel Wharton, I am wounded, I am wounded; have I a friend in this world?" The Texian drums beat assembly and the Texians, with their prisoners, marched back across the field.

Aftermath

Houston was asleep on his left side, lying on a blanket with his head against the oak tree, where he had made his simple camp the night before. His right ankle was shattered by a ball and was dressed as well as the conditions allowed. Some kind-hearted Texian had strung a rope around him so as to prevent their commander from being stepped on by passers-by. He would awake from time to time and weave a garland of laurel, then go back to sleep, which was his only succor from the pain. Just before noon, a group of Texians brought a prisoner up to their commander. Houston was wakened when the prisoner knelt and took his hand. The prisoner stated, that he was "Antonio Lopez de Santa Anna, President of Mexico, who surrendered himself as a prisoner."

Houston showed no emotion and took his hand back from the man and returned it to his breast. Santa Anna continued, "He was born to no uncommon destiny who was the conqueror of the Napoleon of Mexico. For, the same troops who yesterday fled in dismay and terror at your first fire, the day before the united efforts of myself and officers could scarcely restrain from attacking you; they were old soldiers, fought bravely with me in Zacatecas; were familiar with, and had been fearless of danger in all its shapes. It was destiny. And now it remains for you to be generous to the vanquished." Houston replied, coolly, "You should have remembered that at the Alamo."

Juan Almonte

Juan Almonte was born the bastard son of Mexican federalist revolutionary Father José María Morelos y Pavón, and an Indian, Brigida Almonte, on May 15, 1803. Mexican folklore records that Fr. Morelos y Pavón was marching with his soldiers past a village, when an Indian woman appeared and held up a baby boy, declaring that the priest was the father of the child. Allegedly Morelos y Pavón, embarrassed, dismissed her by waving her off with the word *"Almonte"*—"to the mountains"—and that is the legend of his name. Whether the story is true or not will never be known, but at some point the rebel priest assumed responsibility for the boy and sent him to be educated in America amongst expatriate Mexican republicans. His father's execution in December 1815 ended Almonte's education and he began clerking in New Orleans.

When Mexico achieved independence, Almonte returned to his native country from Nacogdoches, Texas, where he had been working, and was appointed to the staff of Don José Felix Trespalacios, headquartered in Texas. In 1824 he was assigned to Great Britain as a member of the Mexican Legation and was largely responsible for Mexico's first commercial agreement with a foreign nation.

In 1830 while working as a newspaper editor, he criticized President Anastasio Bustamente for allowing foreign intrigue into the new republic and was forced into hiding. This brought him into contact with Antonio López de Santa Anna Perez de Lebron.

From his ignominious birth he became involved in the final Mexican revolution and allied himself with the forces for independence from Spain and finally with the nationalist-centralist faction of Mexican politics.

Santa Anna sent him to inspect Texas in 1834 (the only official Mexican report from this period) to determine the potential for Texas as an agricultural and industrial holding and, possibly, for colonial insurrection. His instructions were in two parts, one public and the other secret. The public articles consisted of seven points. For the first, he was to listen and relate any and all colonists' complaints. The second, third and fourth articles concerned his accounting,

Father José María Morelos y Pavón, c. 1814. Father Morelos became the senior revolutionary leader after the execution of Father Hidalgo. This painting is probably by an Indian artist and shows the warrior-priest carrying vestments of both vocations, combining them into one, in a tradition that is purely Mexican. Oddly enough, his largely land-reform-based revolution was replaced by a later revolution of sorts led by his illegitimate son, Juan Almonte, who would begin as a centralist and later became a royalist. (Museo Nacional de Historia, Mexico,)

if inquired, of Texas' potential as a territory. In the sixth point, he was "to make other explanations which may be necessary and of which mention is not made through the pressure of time; [the government] trusting in the integrity of Sr. Almonte and hoping that he would know to reconcile the interests of the colonists with those of the Republic of which they are an integral part." In other words, he was given discretion to

Colonel Juan Nepomuceno Almonte, c. 1830, by Carlos Paris. Chief of Staff of the Mexican Army of Operations for Santa Anna, he left a wonderfully detailed journal that is arguably the single most important primary document from the Mexican perspective. (Author's collection; *Mexico: su tiempo de nacer, 1750–1821*)

say whatever he needed to keep the colonists calm. The seventh and final instruction concerned his response if asked about Stephen Austin, who was still in prison,

"[Austin] remains arrested only because he is accused of having wanted to excite a rebellion in the colonies against the Government of Mexico; but that it is believed that he will be liberated and that he will return to the enjoyment of a peaceful citizenship."

The second and secret portion contained 12 articles that required Almonte to assess everything from the mood of the colonies, the size of their militia and numbers of armaments, to who were the men of influence. He was to return to Mexico City and deliver his report in person.

Aside from the skullduggery, Almonte's inventory of ports, populations, rivers, towns and soil types is superbly succinct and at the same time, informative. Interspersed with the valuable details of the flora and country's potential, he wrote a warning to his superiors in Mexico District Federal (D.F.), "the climate in Texas is perfectly adaptable for the people of [northern] Europe, and the [ir] immigration is so considerable that in less than ten years the [American] population has multiplied five times. Finally, Texas is the most valuable possession that the [Mexican] Republic has, and God grant that our neglect does not cause us to lose so precious a part of our territory."

Almonte remained meticulous, thorough and brief. He served as Santa Anna's Chief of Staff during the Texian War of Independence, and kept a daily journal beginning in February 1836 and ending a few days before the Mexican's defeat at San Jacinto. In the entire journal he made no ideological commentary. He neglected to record the inter-staff quibbling and backstabbing so common among his peers in that army, which is rare in an officer, especially one so loyal to Santa Anna. Throughout the war, he recorded the weather (it never rained during the Alamo siege), and various troop and supply issues consistent with a chief of staff's duties. His last journal sentence on March 6 was, "I was robbed by our soldiers." A traditional robbery is unthinkable, and it is more likely he felt he had been disappointed by their

conduct in some respect, possibly in the summary execution of Texian prisoners. His journal is possibly the single most important historical record of the war, and coupled with his 1834 Statistical Report, he has proved his worth to future generations, if not as a soldier and statesman, than at least as a recorder of history.

While pursuing the retreating Texian Army, Santa Anna sent Almonte to New Washington to capture the rebel government. Almonte and 50 dragoons arrived as the rowboat carried interim President David G. Burnet and his wife from the Morgan Plantation warehouse to the Texas schooner *Flash*, anchored about one-quarter mile (0.4 km) from the shore in Galveston Bay. Burnet had desired that the flatboat hauling cargo out to the schooner be used to transport his entire party, horses included. But a Texian came riding into town warning that the Mexicans were just behind him. Burnet had no time to load the flatboat, so a small rowboat was commandeered. One of the *soldados* managed to touch Burnet with his lance, but the boat was too far from shore, and Burnet was uninjured. The dragoons raised their weapons to fire at the fleeing politician, but Almonte halted their fire and admonished his *soldados* never to fire on women. Burnet had been within easy musket range and would no doubt have been killed or wounded, but with Almonte, humanity overrode expediency. Burnet and his escort arrived safely at Anahuac and went on to Galveston Island. It is impossible to determine how the Texian War of Independence would have turned out had Almonte captured the Texian president rather than the Texians capturing his.

He commanded the Mexican right at San Jacinto, comprised of three *cazadore* companies, and after they broke he was seen swimming Peggy Lake with one hand, the other holding his sword out of the water. During the slaughter Almonte gathered several officers around himself, "Gentlemen, you see that our men will not fight, they are panic stricken; let us get them together and surrender them." His timely leadership and

Juan Almonte during the 1850s when he served
as Mexican Minister to Great Britain or the United
States. No doubt one of the medals he wears is from
the Texas Campaign. His Indian features are more
prominent here than in the portrait 20 years earlier.
(Benson Latin American Collection, University of Texas
at Austin)

cool head no doubt kept these *soldados* from
the butcher's bill that day. At dusk he
surrendered himself and 250 *soldados* on the
southwest side of the battlefield, near the
Old Washington Road. Gen. Thomas
Jefferson Rusk, Texas Secretary of War, took

charge of the prisoners and recorded this meeting with Almonte. "It was probably Almonte whom I saw before me. I therefore observed to him [in Spanish]. 'You must be Colonel Almonte.' He replied in English, 'You speak [Spanish] well.' I then rode up to him and gave him my hand, saying to him, 'It affords me great pleasure to see you, Colonel.' With great presence of mind and his customary politeness he responded, 'The pleasure is reciprocated.'"

One of his guards, a *Tejano*, who was not so hospitable as Rusk, said to the prisoners in their native tongue, "Now you shall see, contemptible and faithless assassins, if you do not pay with your vile blood for your murders at the Alamo and La Bahia. The time has come when the just cause that we defended triumphs over you; you shall pay with you heads for the arson, robberies, and depredations that you have committed in our country."

Almonte remained with Santa Anna during his captivity and served as his translator during the negotiations. He was friendly and courteous to his captors, which must have had some impact on the resolution of his president's fate.

He became Minister of War in 1840 in the cabinet of President Anastacio Bustamente. In July General Urrea and several *soldados* met Almonte on the street, demanded his sword and announced that President Bustamente was to be placed under arrest. Almonte drew his blade and fought through the *soldados*. Once safe, he quickly organized forces to suppress the revolution, although another revolution that fall eventually overthrew the Bustamente government.

Almonte became destitute and earned his income by science lecturing.

When Santa Anna returned to power in 1841, Almonte was named Minister to the United States and once again he became involved in the affairs of Texas. In November of 1843, he wrote the U.S. Secretary of State and declared Mexico's intent for war if the United States annexed Texas. In his letter, he reminded the secretary that the revolution had been caused, at least in part, by U.S. intervention. He made a further argument that when the U.S. had recognized Mexican independence from Spain, that recognition extended to Mexican rule over the Texas province. He reminded the government that regardless of U.S. goals in the region, Mexicans would not be deterred from what was rightfully theirs. If the U.S. Congress voted for annexation, he would immediately return to Mexico, sever diplomatic ties and help prepare Mexico for a war against the United States. Unwilling to become embroiled in another war, America decided against annexing the Republic of Texas at that time.

Almonte continued to work as a diplomat and in subsequent years was twice minister to Great Britain, and minister to the United States again in 1853. While he was in Europe, he gained sympathy for the Mexican monarchists and supported foreign intervention in Mexico to restore the throne. He returned home in 1862 with French soldiers. He was named *"El Jefe Supremo,"* and President of the French Executive Council by the French government. He was exiled after the failure of French intervention and died in Paris on March 21, 1869, aged 65.

The Jacksonian era

"To the south, the Union has one point of contact with the Mexican Empire, where one day serious wars may well develop. But for a long time to come the backwards state of [Mexican] civilization, the degeneration of its morals, and its extreme poverty will stand in the way of any hope of achieving high status among nations. As for the European powers, distance reduces any threat they represent."

Alexis de Tocqueville,
La Démocratie en Amérique

De Tocqueville's *La Démocratie en Amérique*, written in 1835, was a penetrating political observation of the United States, and his words about the southern U.S. borders and Mexico were uncannily accurate. In one of the appendices he discussed the particular geographic challenges the European powers would have in North American involvement: "It is true that European powers can wage great maritime wars against the Union but it is always easier and less dangerous to undertake a maritime war than a land war…As for land wars, it is clear that the European people offer no threat to the United States."

While the threat of land war was minimal, especially after the bloody wars of North American conquest during the 18th century, the risk of foreign political interference in Texas from the United States and other countries was a factor in the Texian War of Independence.

United States

The United States was a "young" nation and as such was perpetually alert to the dangers of foreign intervention in the first quarter of the 19th century. It was this fear that produced the Monroe Doctrine on December 2, 1823, sponsored through Congress by Secretary of State John Quincy Adams. The doctrine existed primarily to discourage and prevent further European interference in New World countries, although when Texas declared its independence from Mexico, the Doctrine carried little if any international weight, since Texas was involved in a war for independence not from a European nation, but from Mexico. It would not be used as an argument for Texan annexation until 1845, when the new U.S. President, James K. Polk, exploited it.

If the Monroe Doctrine was the "legal" precedent for preventing further European involvement, then the concept of Manifest Destiny was the moral covenant. The term first appeared in the *Democratic Review* in 1845 and argued for the U.S. mission to extend its systems across the continent. Neither the Monroe Doctrine nor the theory of Manifest Destiny applied directly to the Texian situation in 1835–36, but their implications were widely understood and discussed by the participants in the Revolution.

Andrew Jackson, the seventh President of the United States, was an expansionist if for no other reason than to deny European powers the use of the North American continent. Several of the personalities of the Texian War for Independence had, at one time or another, been in his camp, notably Congressman David Crockett and Governor Sam Houston who, like Jackson, both hailed from Tennessee. Because of this connection to the White House, there are many who regard the Texian War as one giant Jacksonian land grab. However, there exists no evidence of martial or material support from either Jackson or the U.S. government to suggest that they sponsored or financed the Texian War. Having said that, the

Andrew Jackson (1767–1845), the first American president who truly seemed to be one of the people. Brave, honest and highly competent, he enjoyed a distinguished military career before turning to politics. (Library of Congress, Prints and Photographs Division LC-USZ62-5099)

Texians' moral code—what they fought for— was undoubtedly influenced by Jacksonian aims. It was the age of the "white poor" and Jackson was the first of their kind to win the presidency, having achieved his status thanks to his own ambitions and abilities, and without recourse to anyone else's money. He was the model for the American white male during the middle years of the 19th century, so much so that the years from 1815 until the U.S.–Mexican War are known as the Jacksonian era.

One major reason, other than *détente*, for the United States' distance from the intrigues with Mexico during the Texian War, was their overwhelming involvement with the former Spanish territory of Florida and the Seminole occupants. The Seminole were not a separate tribe, but more than likely a southern band of Creek Indians. Probably driven south by the French, who had destroyed a large warlike tribe when they controlled the Mississippi, they migrated into Florida from their ancestral home in the Mississippi river valley in about 1721. Florida had been a Spanish colony until 1763, when the territory was ceded to England, but in 1783 Florida returned to the Spanish Crown. Following the War of 1812, Spanish Florida was annexed by the United States and several treaties were signed with the Seminole. The first was the Treaty of Camp Moultrie in 1823, which stated that all slaves who had sought safety with the Indians were to be returned, the Seminoles would be relocated to the Indian Territory (then Arkansas) and the government would reimburse the Seminole for all their property for 20 years. Since the treaty did not specify when the relocation would occur, the natives saw no reason to hurry from their land and assumed the U.S. would pay them for the next generation.

This misunderstanding had to be repaired. In 1832, the Treaty of Payne's Landing was signed by 15 of the southern bands, but three years later many of them would not recognize it and refused to relocate. Both this treaty and the earlier one caused grief among the growing number of "adopted" Seminoles— runaway slaves—who had made a new life with the Indians and were none too friendly towards the Americans. Several of the bands began making ready for war.

In June of 1835, near Hogtown (now Gainesville), seven Seminole left the reservation to hunt. On June 19 they encountered some whites and an altercation occurred. Two Seminole died and three whites were wounded. On August 6 a uniformed mail carrier was murdered and mutilated by Seminoles, probably in revenge for the June incident, on the Fort King Road near the Hillsborough Bridge.

In late December 1835, General Clinch and his command, in desperate need of provisions, left Fort King for his plantation. A dispatch was sent to Fort Brooke (Tampa) ordering fresh troops to immediately relieve the garrison. As soon as the soldiers marched away, Seminoles attacked the sutler's cabin and killed the five men who had remained. At Fort Brooke, the courier from Clinch arrived and the message was interpreted that Fort King was under siege; a relief column was dispatched forthwith.

Major (Brevet) Francis L. Dade commanded a relief troop of around 100 men, including infantry and artillery. The march to Fort King was dangerous. In the past, the Seminole had preferred the hammocks (the canopy forest)

for their ambuscades. The column remained alert until they had passed through the jungle-like terrain and arrived at the Pine Barrens. Rain and cold weather forced the men into their greatcoats and they carried their weapons and wore their accoutrements under their coats to keep it dry.

The Seminole chiefs, Micanopy, Alligator and Juniper, trailed the column and then waited for them at Wahoo Swamp with approximately 180 braves. As the soldiers marched past, the Seminoles fired, killing or wounding half the command with this volley. Dade died first. The Seminole then prepared to leave, having fought what they believed was a successful ambush. Then they noticed the soldiers taking felled trees and making a small triangular fort with the logs, so they renewed their attack until 2:00 PM when the tiny fort fell silent. The bodies were mutilated and only three soldiers escaped back to Fort Brooke. This was the beginning of the 2nd Seminole War, which

The Pioneer Cowpen, by Friedrich Richard Petri, c. 1853. This painting depicts life as most Texians would have preferred—peaceful and routine. (Center for American History, the University of Texas at Austin)

An engraving of Charles Gilbert Stuart's 1839 portrait of Colonel David Crockett holding up his hat and rifle with two dogs. This depicts Tennessee Congressman David Crockett as he wanted to appear, although the painting was done in Washington and all the effects borrowed. The clothing and accoutrements may not be Crockett's but they are certainly contemporary. (From an original painting at the University of Texas at Austin, Library of Congress Prints and Photographs Division LC-USZ62-93521)

lasted until 1846 and was the costliest Indian War the U.S. ever engaged in. As the U.S. was too involved with Florida to take an active role in Texas, so is it that Dade's Massacre (the third worst by natives against U.S. Regulars) is hardly known by most Americans today.

Historically, the battle had the misfortune of occurring just ten weeks prior to the fall of the Alamo. Americans can remember the Alamo, but most have forgotten all about Dade and his ill-fated command. It was deserters from this war who "volunteered" for the Texian cause during the San Jacinto campaign and doubtless provided a trained cadre for Houston to build an army around.

The Texian Republican Army was primarily a homegrown one. The war's duration and distance from the main population centers of the United States prevented a timely and large reinforcement from the "old country." The majority of volunteers who trickled in during the war

A Seminole attack on a block house, possibly on the Withlacoochee River in December 1835. It was this war with the Seminole that prevented greater U.S. involvement in the Texian Revolution. (Library of Congress Prints and Photographs Division LC-USZC4-2398)

proper did not arrive until after the Treaties of Velasco.

European interest

Although by the 1830s the European powers largely accepted the status quo in North America, enterprising governments watched the events in Texas with interest to see whether any political or commercial advantages would open up to them. Great Britain was especially keen to gain another commercial lodgment in North America, and Texian diplomats contacted Great Britain as soon as the Declaration of Independence was signed. There were two British officials stationed in Galveston, Texas, during the 1840s, Chargé d'affaires Charles Elliot and Consul William Kennedy.

"*Every* [Texian] *man is a marksman and carries his rifle*," wrote Jos. T. Crawford, the British vice-consul to Mexico immediately after the revolution. He penned numerous detailed reports to the British Foreign Office, as well as to his superiors at the British embassy in Mexico City. Instead of establishing diplomatic relations with the new nation of Texas, Crawford seems to

have set about gathering useful intelligence, noting, for example, all the ports along the Texas coast, both actual and potential, and commenting on their usefulness in a naval or martial capacity. Along with this he reported that the majority of shipping was coming from the United States, which by itself should not be surprising as that was the closest trading neighbor, but he was particular about the passengers; it was Americans that were arriving on these ships.

Understanding that the British were keen to gain another source of cheap raw cotton in addition to that supplied by the southern states of the United States, Crawford also took an interest in the cotton exportation. He reported that the average number of bales exported had been 60,000, but less seed had been sown during the War of Independence, so the 1836–37 crop would decline to around 30,000 bales.

He defined for his superiors a synopsis of the Texian War of Independence and the structure of the Texas government to include militia and army numbers and the ability to mobilize to meet a threat. He was enough impressed with the sad state of Texian military affairs to correctly predict that the "... [Texian] *Territory will never be subject to her* [Mexican] *countrol* [sic]." While he reported pleasantly enough on the Texians,

not all were as impressed with him. The *Telegraph and Texas Register* reported, "The object of this gentleman's visit to Texas, is we understand to investigate the civil and political condition of the country and report to the British government."

The French interest in Texas was also long-standing. René Robert Cavelier, Sieur de La Salle, claimed Texas for France in 1685 and fueled Spanish paranoia for the next century or at least until the French Revolution manifested itself and gave the Spanish Crown a larger threat than Franco-incursion; that of a popular revolt. In 1818 100-plus French émigrés settled on the Trinity River and called their "colony" Champ d'Aisle ("field of asylum"), declaring that they would pursue agricultural and commercial interests. Led by former general Charles Lallemand, this newest European incursion into the New World alarmed both Spain and the United States. Hearing that a column of Spanish royalists was marching toward their Eden, the French moved to Galveston Island and lived amongst the pirates of Jean Lafitte. Disease, Indians, duels, assassinations and overwork defeated the erstwhile colonists before they could be re-exiled by the Spanish. This was the last French attempt at colonization north of the Río Grande.

Angelina Dickenson, "Babe of the Alamo"

Angelina Dickenson, known as the "Babe of the Alamo," was the baby who survived the brutal slaughter at the Alamo and spent the rest of her life living in its shadow. Her blacksmith father and illiterate 22-year-old mother arrived at DeWitt's Colony, Gonzales, Coahuila y Texas, on February 20, 1831. Her connection to the Alamo is a result of her mother being robbed and possibly raped by East Texas volunteers passing through Gonzales, while her father was at the battle of Béxar in December 1835 and died defending the Alamo.

Angelina Elizabeth Dickenson was born December 14, 1834, after five years of marriage, to Almeron and Susannah Arabella Dickenson. Her father was a farrier and had some experience with artillery, possibly in his native Tennessee or with regular U.S. forces. They may have run their home as a boarding house and may have also operated a hattery in the small town.

After the war of independence, the birth of the new Texan republic became invested with symbolic imagery and Angelina came to represent the new life that sprang from the destruction of the war. As the only Anglo child to survive the Alamo, Angelina lived her life with the moniker "Babe of the Alamo."

Fighting the centralists in Béxar in the winter of 1835, Dickenson soon sent for his family to join him in San Antonio, where he must have believed they would be safe. Once in Béxar, the family lived in the Músquiz house on Main Plaza across from the San Fernando church. Ramon Músquiz hired Susannah to cook and clean for his boarders, who included David Crockett. On February 23 as the Mexicans arrived in Béxar, Almeron rushed to collect his family and rode up to the house, saying, "Give me the baby, jump up behind and ask me no questions." The direct route to the Alamo was already

Angelina Dickenson, the "Babe of the Alamo." This image was probably taken around the time of her first marriage in 1851. She would never remember the events that made her famous, but the overwhelming circumstances of her infancy, when she was depicted as the innocent child at the center of the Texan creation myth, probably hastened her demise later in life. It must have been hard being held up as an example of perfection to an entire region. (DRT)

blocked and the Dickensons had to travel north of town then ford the river near the sugar mill. Once safe in the Alamo, the mother and daughter were housed in the sacristy of the church with the other non-combatants. Upon arrival, Susannah had so forgotten herself that Ana Salizar Esparza had to care for the young woman and her child. Angelina must have seen her father often as he was assigned the church battery, only feet from the sacristy's door. It is possible that she saw him die as well.

After the battle, a Mexican officer came to the door and asked for her mother. Músquiz had doubtless asked the officer to look to her safety. As the mother and child were being escorted out of the church and through the *campo santo*, Susannah was wounded in the right calf by an errant musket ball.

The Dickensons were taken back to their former quarters at the Músquiz house, where they were interviewed by Santa Anna and given two dollars and a blanket. He also liberated his indentured servant, Ben, to escort them and he sent a letter to Houston to warn the Texians of his intent. Legend has it that Santa Anna wanted to rear Angelina as his own, and although this story is popular in Texas, the source for this account is unknown. It is an interesting thought to

The Death of Dickenson, c. 1844, by Theodore Gentilz. Almeron Dickenson kneels and holds his daughter before him as he attempts to surrender. This is a stylized image of a moment that never happened and was probably confused by Gentilz with a defender jumping with a child from the back of the church during the final battle. The soldados appear in a mix of winter and summer fatigue uniforms. The building in the background is the southernmost end of the convento. (Daughters of the Republic of Texas Library at the Alamo)

imagine her growing up as minor royalty, probably in better circumstances than she subsequently enjoyed. After a brief respite so that Susannah could recover from her wound, the threesome left on the Gonzales Road, passing the smoldering pyres where Almeron Dickenson's charred remains mingled with those of his comrades. East of the town and near the Cibolo Creek crossing, the party discovered William B. Travis's slave, Joe, who joined the procession.

Outside Gonzales they over-nighted at the Bruno Farm, with mother and daughter staying inside, and the two blacks sleeping in the woods. They stayed a few days and then set out again for Gonzales. Deaf Smith and two others who were conducting reconnaissance for Houston to determine if the Alamo still held, discovered the refugees. Susannah's presence gave them their information and the three Texians escorted the survivors to Gonzales.

Houston ordered the Texian Republican Army to retreat to the east and burned Gonzales; Susannah's home was fired along

with the rest. The Bruno family again took in mother and daughter to Nash Creek. After the revolution, the Brunos returned to Gonzales but Susannah and Angelina remained in the Nash Creek area.

Despite their status as dependents of a deceased Alamo defender, the Republic of Texas never provided financial support for

Susannah Arabella Dickenson Williams Herring appears here in mourning garb, probably after the death of her third husband in 1843. The horror her eyes saw through the entire revolution is scarcely evident here. Although aged only in her early forties at the time of this photograph, this was the second time circumstance obliged her to don mourning clothes for the death of a husband. (Adina DeZavala Papers, Center for American History, the University of Texas at Austin)

either Susannah or Angelina. The only property they received was the original league (land) provided under Mexican law. From time to time the Texan Republic and later the state legislatures would discuss money for Angelina and her mother, but to no avail.

With no income, nor potential for income, Susannah married John Williams on November 27, 1837. Her second marriage lasted only four months—she received a divorce on the grounds of cruelty, charging Williams with causing Susannah a miscarriage and of abuse of Angelina. On December 20, 1838, she married Francis P. Herring, a water hauler in Houston. The marriage ended five years later when Herring died of alcoholism. Angelina's mother was a widow again and by the age of nine, Angelina had already known three fathers and lost two of them. Angelina was 13 when her mother married again, to Peter Bellows. The family established another boarding house and one of their frequent customers was John Maynard Griffith, a farmer and steamboat captain. He was a strong Christian and Susannah deemed him acceptable to court her by now comely 16-year-old daughter. Perhaps Susannah felt this successful and disciplined man would provide her daughter with the structure and discipline she had never received as a child. They married on July 8, 1851 and had three children over the next six years—Almeron Dickenson, Susannah Arabella and Joseph Griffith.

Angelina must have felt overcome by the events of life, marriage, children and so many rules. She had always received attention as the "Babe of the Alamo," but precious little discipline. One Texan wrote of her during this time, "She did not look so fresh and attractive as when I had first met her...Her greeting was less cordial and shadows were lurking on the surface of the broad open forehead. An anxious and at times a pained expression would creep over her face, and there was listlessness and signs of languor perceptible in her eyes." Love of life never slowed Angelina, who apparently enjoyed dancing and indulging herself. After

one particularly "great fete" or "blowout" near the community of Cyprus, her husband could tolerate her behavior no more. He sued for and received a divorce. The Baptist preacher who married them later wrote, "Soon the vivacious city girl got tired of her country home and amiable, plodding husband. Alienations, repining and then divorce followed. The mother's heart bled over the ruin of her child's happiness." Angelina's eldest child was remanded to an uncle and Susannah reared the two youngest. While Angelina had been enduring her first marriage, her mother ended her fourth. Peter Bellows was granted a divorce on June 15, 1857. He had accused Susannah of adultery and abandonment.

In Galveston, Angelina became the common-law wife of James Britton until the beginning of the Civil War in 1861 when he returned to his native Tennessee and became an officer in the 4th Regiment. Before he left, she gave him Travis's ring that he had placed around her neck the night before the final assault on the Alamo. From Galveston she moved to New Orleans and married Oscar Holmes in 1864 by whom she had a daughter, Sallie. This marriage ended in divorce as well. Sometime during this period her mother journeyed to New Orleans to recover or at least redirect her daughter. By this time, Angelina had embraced the life of a courtesan and even though her mother may have engaged in this trade from time to time between husbands, Angelina seems to have given over to the lifestyle entirely. Susannah's trip was unsuccessful but she did take custody of Sallie and returned with her to Austin. The mother and daughter never saw each other again. Angelina began going by the name of Emma Britton, perhaps to wash away a name that was forever surrounded by death or perhaps because James Britton had brought her the only happiness she had ever known. After some time she returned to Galveston and died there in 1869 at the age of 34 of a uterine hemorrhage. The 1900 Galveston tidal surge likely washed away her grave.

"Take them dead Mexicans off my league"

After San Jacinto some 600 decaying corpses littered the area around Peggy Lake, the numbers gradually decreasing to the mid-field area. Near the breastworks, a Texian took gold and silver teeth from the dead and another visitor recorded that "the pockets of every one had been turned out in plunder." The Texians were as unconcerned over safety as they were over propriety. They examined ammunition and ordnance with lit pipes in their mouths. One of them recovered a pistol from the ground and accidentally discharged the weapon, causing some 20 ammunition boxes to explode, and setting the knee-high grass on fire. The nearby prisoners were evacuated, but the fire was soon brought under control.

There still remained a problem of the bodies. Should the *soldados* be forced to bury their comrades? Houston asked Santa Anna's advice, who answered that he "found incremation a ready solution."

The San Jacinto battlefield extended over the McCormick Ranch, and when Irish colonist Peggy McCormick returned she was aghast at her property's condition. She asked Houston "if he was going to take them dead Mexicans off my league." Houston said he was not, and in "mock seriousness" told her "your land will be famed in history." The rather more practical Peggy answered back, "To devil with your glorious history, take off your stinking Mexicans."

After their introductions on the 21st, Houston met with Santa Anna for two hours; Deaf Smith sat nearby with his hand cupped around his ear, leaning forward to hear the discussion. Following Houston's orders to Santa Anna, Ramón Caro prepared instructions for Filisola, and Smith was assigned to carry it to the Italian. He and two others departed and on April 23, between Harrisburg and Fort Bend, they captured a Mexican courier. They showed him the orders for Filisola, and then released him to carry the message himself. Smith and his party followed the dispatch rider at a distance, but later that same day they encountered another Mexican dressed nicely and carrying a pitcher of water and an ear of corn. The prisoner was carried back to San Jacinto. Along the way, Smith questioned the prisoner. Did he fight in the battle? Yes, he did. How did he escape? After dark on a horse, which he had to abandon at a burned bridge. Have you seen General Cós? No, the prisoner replied. "I am Deaf Smith, and I want to find General Cós. He offered $1,000 for my head, and if I find him I will cut his head off and send it to Mexico." No doubt this reply shook the prisoner. Smith learned when he reached the Texian camp that his well-dressed prisoner was Cós.

The Mexican retreat

After his capture, Santa Anna ordered his remaining forces to march to Guadalupe Victoria. Prior to the arrival of his missive, and not being sure of the Texian forces facing them, Filisola ordered a retreat to the west bank of the Colorado River. Deaf Smith found Filisola on the San Bernard River and returned to Houston with the news that the Mexican forces were retreating. Always cautious, Houston sent two companies of cavalry to make contact with the Mexicans and provide a screen for the Texian forces.

The Mexican army remained where it had been upon the defeat and capture of Santa Anna. They were deployed along the southern bank of the Río Brazos with second-in-command (now commander) Filisola at Old Fort, Col. Salas at Columbia, Gen. Urrea at Brazoria and Col. Andrade at

Béxar. Even without the missive from Santa Anna, Filisola at Fort Bend already knew the overall situation. The rearguard commander of Cós's column had heard the battle from his location and received fleeing *soldados*. Col. Mariano Garcia wrote a message, dismounted and sent a *soldado* on his horse to report to Filisola; he reached him early on the 22nd. Filosola retreated with Gaona's column of 1,000 *soldados* to Mrs Powell's Tavern, concerned over the Texians continuing the offensive. Late in the afternoon, Filisola sent orders to Urrea to rejoin the main body at the tavern.

Filisola ordered all 4,000 *soldados* to mass at Mrs. Powell's home near Brazoria, intending to regroup, refit and continue the campaign at a later date. For now, however, a strategic withdrawal was necessary. What followed was not pleasant and many officers would later blame Filisola for the eventual retreat. Urrea later claimed that he had argued for the resumption of offensive

The Surrender of Santa Anna, by Henry Huddle (1886). Houston leans against the "surrender oak" with his back to Buffalo Bayou. He is surrounded by eager Texians, roaring for the summary execution of Santa Anna. Santa Anna appears, hat in hand, standing by himself with his former chief of staff, Almonte, standing away from his president. Houston was actually wounded in the other leg and the rope tied around him to prevent people treading on him is missing. The clothing is anachronistic and is more representative of the 1880s than that noontime on April 22 when the moment actually occurred. (Texas State Library and Archives Commission)

operations against the Texians. He recalled, "Can the success of such a combination be doubted? It seemed certain that Houston had only about 720 men and they had an equal number of prisoners to guard. Under such circumstances, it is impossible to believe that nearly 3,000 men, all in fighting trim, could not have obtained a complete victory?"

It is only fair to point out that Filisola, though senior and legally the commander, offered to step aside to allow a native, rather than an Italian to command the army. Urrea did not step forward. Filisola reorganized the forces into three brigades, the first under Gen. Gaona, the second under Gen. Tolsa and the third under Gen. Urrea. A reserve column was organized under the command of Gen. Ramírez y Sesma, who was also named as second-in-command to Filisola. In short, the Mexicans still had an army of over 4,000 that could have made short work of the mob of undisciplined rebels relaxing at Buffalo Bayou. The Mexicans began their retreat on April 26 amid heavy rains that turned the ground to almost impenetrable mud. Men sank up to their knees and began to discard cumbersome

General of Division Vicente Filisola, c. 1835. Santa Anna's second-in-command during the Texian War of Independence, he assumed control of the centralist army after Santa Anna's surrender. He followed his commander's orders and retreated south of the Río Grande. Severely criticized for his actions, he was later exonerated by a court of inquiry. He wrote a two-volume *History of the Texian War* that is invaluable. (Benson Collection, the University of Texas at Austin)

equipment, even, as time went by, their weapons. Many succumbed to dysentery and the morale of the already beleaguered army sank even lower.

Peace negotiations

On May 5 Houston turned command of the Texian army over to Secretary of War Thomas Rusk. Rusk agreed to assume command, but only temporarily. On May 7 the cabinet, along with the senior Mexican prisoners, was to travel to Galveston. Houston was still bedridden and his condition had worsened. His surgeon became concerned that he would get an infection if better care were not given immediately. As Houston was being carried up the gangplank of *Yellowstone*, Burnet, himself a passenger onboard, stopped the procession and declared the ship was not available for civilian transportation. The

A contemporary cartoon depicting the Texian victory at San Jacinto, entitled *Houston, Santa Anna & Cós* which reflects the strong anti-Mexican feeling in the United States after the slaughter at the Alamo and Goliad. Santa Anna (center) bows and offers his sword to Houston, saying, "I consent to remain your prisoner, most excellent sir!! Me no Alamo!!" His subordinate follows suit. Houston, clad in buckskins and holding a musket, says, "You are two bloody villains, and to treat you as you deserve, I ought to have you shot as an example! Remember the Alamo and Fannin!" (Library of Congress, Prints and Photographs Division LC-USZ62-1273)

ship's Captain, J.E. Ross, responded, "This ship is not sailing, unless General Houston is on it." Burnet backed down and Houston was evacuated to New Orleans via Galveston.

Meanwhile, interim President David G. Burnet had begun negotiations with Santa Anna. On May 14, 1836, Presidents Burnet and Santa Anna signed the Treaties of Velasco. There were two documents, one for public consumption and the other secret.

The public treaty contained ten articles.

1. Santa Anna agreed not to again take up arms, nor influence others to do so, against Texas.

2. Hostilities were to cease immediately.

3. Those Mexican forces still in Texas would retreat south of the Río Grande (thus designating the Río Grande as the southern-most border of Texas).

4. The retreating Mexican army would not make use of private property without the owner's consent and would pay remuneration.

5. All confiscated colonists' property would be restored by the Mexicans.

6. The troops from the opposing armies would not make contact and would remain at least five leagues apart.

7. The Mexican Army would not delay in their retreat.

8. The remaining Mexican military leadership in Texas would be made aware of the constraints of the treaty.

9. All prisoners of war would be returned to their countrymen.

10. Santa Anna was to be sent to Vera Cruz as soon as possible.

The secret portion (conditional upon execution of the ten public articles) consisted of six articles, among them the immediate release of Santa Anna if he used his influence for Mexican recognition of Texas independence; the Mexican cabinet was to receive a Texas commerce delegation to develop a treaty of commerce between the two republics; and a further specification that the Texas southern boundary extend no further than the Río Grande.

Since the Texas Army refused Santa Anna's liberation, the secret portion of the Treaties of Velasco was never fulfilled.

Once the Treaties of Velasco were concluded, Rusk, who had always wanted to pursue and attack the remaining Mexican forces, was allowed to follow them but undertake no offensive action. He would instead function as a security escort until the Mexicans were out of Texas. The Texian Republican Army followed first west and then southwest, first with the cavalry companies of Henry Karnes and Juan Seguín commanded by Sidney Sherman.

On May 17 the Mexican army assembled at Goliad to await Col. Andrade marching from Béxar. The torrential rains had delayed his march. On May 25 Col. Benjamin Highsmith, Maj. McIntire and Capt. Henry Teal arrived at the *presidio* with two uniformed escorts. They delivered to Filisola the Treaty of Velasco, which Filisola signed and honored. On May 26 the Mexican army began its ignominious retreat from Texas.

The Texian army halted at Goliad. Just outside the former Fort Defiance were the largely unburied corpses of their murdered comrades, picked over for eight weeks by turkey buzzards, feral dogs, and prairie wolves. On June 3 Rusk ordered a funeral for 9:00 AM the following day. Sherman was to be in command of the parade, with the 1st Artillery leading the procession, which included survivors of the executions who marched as mourners. Sometime after 9:00 AM, when the procession arrived at the gravesite, Rusk delivered his remarks.

"Fellow soldiers: In the order of Providence we are this day called upon to pay the last sad offices of respect to the remains of the noble and heroic band, who, battling for our sacred

Interim President David G. Burnet. He despised Houston and constantly prodded him during the 1836 campaign. He was almost captured or killed at New Washington, but for the chivalry of Colonel Juan Almonte, who would not allow his *soldados* to fire for fear of hitting Burnet's wife, the first lady. A man of conflicting mores, he would later risk his life to protect the captured Santa Anna and became an ardent Unionist during the American Civil War. (Center for American History, the University of Texas at Austin)

rights, have fallen beneath the ruthless hand of a tyrant. Their chivalrous conduct entitles them to the heartfelt gratitude of the people of Texas. Without any further interest in the country than that which all noble hearts feel at the bare mention of liberty, they rallied to our standard. Relinquishing the ease, peace, and comforts of their homes, leaving behind them all they held dear, their mothers, sisters, daughters, and wives, they subjected themselves to fatigue and privation, and nobly threw themselves between the people of Texas and the legions of Santa Anna. There, unaided by reinforcements and far from help and hope, they battled bravely with the

President-General Antonio López de Santa Anna de
Perez de Lebron by Paul L'Ouvrier. Painted in 1858, the
portrait captures the arrogance and defiance of the man
who dominated Mexican politics in the 19th century.
(Bridgeman Art Library/New York Historical Society)

minions of the tyrant, one to one.
Surrounded in the open prairie by these
fearful odds, cut off from provisions and even
water, they were induced under the sacred
promise of receiving the treatment usual to

prisoners of war, to surrender. They were marched back, and for a week treated with the utmost inhumanity and barbarity. They were marched out of yonder fort under the pretense of getting provisions, and it was not until the firing of musketry and the shrieks of the dying, that they were satisfied of their approaching fate. Some endeavored to make their escape, but they were pursued by the ruthless cavalry and most of them cut down with their swords. A small number of them stand by the grave—a bare remnant of that noble band. Our tribute of respect is due them; is due to the mothers, sisters, and wives who weep their untimely end, that we should mingle our tears with theirs. In that mass of remains and fragments of bones, many a mother might see her son, many a sister or brother, and many a wife her own beloved and affectionate husband. But we have a consolation—yet to offer them: their murderers sank in death on the prairies of San Jacinto, under the appalling words, 'Remember La Bahía.' Many a tender and affectionate woman will remember with tearful eye, 'La Bahía.' But we have another consolation to offer. It is, that while liberty has a habitation and a name, their chivalrous deeds will be handed down upon the bright pages of history. We can still offer another consolation: Santa Anna, the mock hero, the black-hearted murderer, is within our grasp. Yea, and there he must remain, tortured with the keen pain of corroding conscience. He must oft remember La Bahía, and while the names of those whom he murdered shall soar to the highest pinnacle of fame, his shall sink down into the lowest depths of infamy and disgrace."

The sky darkened and a torrent began. At the same time, the three Mexican brigades continued their line of march through flooded roads and ford sites, dragging their cannon and trains with them. It was not the Texians who won at San Jacinto, but the weather that finally defeated the *soldados* and crushed their morale. As far away as the Red River, the word spread. Texas had won the war. Comanches would tell the northernmost colonists that, "Tibo [white man]-Mex get sick and go home. Their horses sick, too."

General Rusk encamped the Texian army at Victoria. He sent out numerous appeals for supplies and recruits because he believed that the war was not yet won and the Mexicans had more than enough forces to take back their former territory. The Burnet government had delegates in the United States attempting to secure just these needs, though it remained to Rusk and his officers the opinion of a re-conquest. The Texian government was cash-poor and it was with land that payment would be made for volunteers and provisions.

Meanwhile, the belated though noble attempts of the interim government were moving too slowly for the Texian officers at Guadalupe Victoria. On May 26 several officers drafted a letter to President Burnet at Velasco: "And now we require that this army be immediately furnished with a sufficiency of such provisions and clothes as the public may possess or can be procured…Unless you take immediate and efficient measures to draft men and enlist regulars, Texas will again be endangered and you will not be excusable…It is well known by whom [Santa Anna] was captured, and at what risk, and we will not permit him to be liberated."

On June 1 Santa Anna and his staff, along with some cabinet secretaries, were boarded on *Invincible*, a Texas warship. Burnet, to his credit, was determined to honor the less-than-public portion of the Velasco Treaties. Santa Anna, much to the displeasure of the Texian Army (now filled with recent immigrants from the United States who had mostly missed the war), was spared and even sent to Washington, D.C., where he visited President Andrew Jackson, and returned to Vera Cruz, Mexico, later that year.

Independence and annexation

"...it is a fundamental mistake to think of Mexico, in this period, or for many years before, as a republic or even a government. It must be understood as a late stage in the breakdown of the Spanish Empire."

Bernard Devoto
(*The Year of Decision: 1846*)

The Texian War of Independence began as a discussion over statehood for the Anglo-populated half-state of Texas. It matured into rebellion for separation and self-government and then developed into a fully-fledged war of independence. The transformation of the Mexican Republic into a dictatorship aided the colonists' movement, as did the subsequent federalist revolts throughout northern Mexico. Coahuila and Zacatecas failed in their rebellions against centralism—the Texian colonists succeeded.

Centralism and federalism were two sides of the republican coin. They do not have to be treated as opposites, but often are. In fact, even in present times these two interpretations represent political parties and ideologies that all ask the same questions—what is the role of government? What is liberty?

To the Anglo-southerner, government's role was to stay far away from him and his kith and kin. In this era of the "white-poor," (with one of them—Andrew Jackson—installed as the United States president), frontiersmen and settlers believed that they could survive quite adequately without government help or interference; their egalitarian motto was "The role of government is not to accomplish good, but refrain from doing evil." Each individual was an emotional descendant of John Locke and Adam Smith, even if most had never heard of either.

The Mexicans viewed government differently. Unlike the U.S. and because of Mexico's remaining royalist sentiments, there was an active political movement to recreate the monarchy in one form or another. These people were centralists and both the military and the Church endorsed them. They were opposed, often at great risk, by the federalists, who believed in the rights of the individual, state and land reform (redistribution), and a greatly reduced role for the Church. Men such as Navarro remained loyal to their conviction of local government, and often placed their life in danger by their actions.

For the decade following the war, the Mexican government concerned itself with regaining her lost territory. In 1842 army forces under the Frenchified-Mexican General Wool captured Béxar. Texas responded with an invasion of Mexico, first to Mier and later to Santa Fé. Mexico's constant threat of war with the U.S. should Texas be annexed, meant that statehood would not be resolved as quickly as some would have liked. But many were happy with Texan autonomy, namely Mirabeau Bonaparte Lamar. An enemy of Houston since the Runaway Scrape, he was nevertheless a hero after his actions at San Jacinto. When he succeeded Houston as president, his foreign policy was first and foremost to remain a republic.

One of the unresolved problems of the War of Texian Independence was the question of the southern border. In the Mexican Constitution of 1824, Texas and Coahuila formed one state, with the intrastate border being the Río Nueces. But since the constitution had been overthrown by the centralist administration of Santa Anna, there was no defined border in Mexican law. The Spaniards had always determined the Río Grande to be the border of Texas, and with the parole of Cós and

Treaties of Velasco both specifying the withdrawal of the army south of the Río Grande, it is obvious the colonists viewed this river and not the Nueces as their southern border. Additionally, there was one Anglo colony south of the Río Nueces, at Corpus Christi. This dispute would eventually be solved by U.S. occupation prior to the U.S–Mexican War.

José Antonio Navarro, one of two *Tejano* signatories of the Texian Declaration of Independence. He had a long history of federalist sentiment and was involved with the Gutierez rebellion in 1812 and 1813. After its failure he fled to Louisiana, but he returned to his native Texas and represented Béxar in the Texas and Coahuila legislature after Mexican independence. In later years he served in numerous positions in the republic's and later state's government. (Barker American History Center, the University of Texas at Austin)

It became Texan governmental policy to create an impassable terrain to prevent invasion from Mexico. El Camino Reale was secure enough (or so they thought, until the Mexicans invaded—twice!), but the coastal road (which Urrea had utilized) went straight up into the center of the populated areas. On August 8, 1836, President Burnet had ordered that the area between the two rivers was to be made into a desert. Texian militia drove all the horses and feral cattle from the region to deny their usage to a potential invasion. The Mexicans called this area *El Desierto Muerto*—"the dead desert."

In Mexico the federalist problem was far from resolved, with the Federalist Wars afflicting northern Mexico from 1838 to 1840. For a time a republic of the Río Grande was established by federalists Antonio Canales and Jesús Cárdenas.

In the United States, the Republic of Texas was viewed as a potential challenge to the balance of power between free and slave states. The northeastern states, in particular, were not pleased by the possibility of another slave state entering the union, and threats of war by Mexico should annexation occur did not sweeten the pot either. However, even the most ardent northeastern abolitionists sympathized with the Texians once the degree of Santa Anna's barbarity become known.

The Mexicans' fear of Texan union with the U.S. was well founded. Regardless of Travis's and others soliloquies on independence, it did not take long for the new republic to court the United States. In November 1836 Texian Minister William H. Wharton aired the republic's desire for annexation. However disappointing to conspiracy theorists who surmise that the Texian War of Independence was a gigantic Jacksonian Land Grab, the U.S. President Andrew Jackson wavered over the annexation offer and Texas withdrew her request on October 12, 1838.

When San Jacinto hero Mirabeau B. Lamar succeeded Houston as president of the Texan republic, he instituted an internal policy to ensure that Texas remained an independent nation. By the end of his term of office he had secured the recognition of several northern European countries, among them Great Britain, Holland and Belgium.

Sam Houston entered into his second term as president in 1841 and began again his efforts to have Texas annexed to his former country. Mexican Minister of Foreign Relations, José Maria de Bocanegra, warned the U.S. Minister to Mexico, Waddy Thompson, in writing:

"That the [government] of Mexico considered as a declaration of war against the Mexican Republic the existence of that accord of the incorporation of Texas into the territory of the United States. The certainty of the fact [of annexation] would suffice that instantly war would be proclaimed [by Mexico], leaving to the civilized world the decision as to the justice of the Mexican people, in a struggle in which they were found so far from provoking."

The threat worked and Houston failed in this attempt to secure annexation, but he was far from finished with trying.

The U.S. Congress approved a resolution inviting Texas to join the union in February 1844 and Texas accepted the invitation on July 4 of the same year. President Tyler signed the resolution one year later. Two days after southern Democrat James K. Polk became the 11th president on March 4, 1845, the Mexican Minister to the United States, Juan Almonte, fulfilled his promise and severed diplomatic relations between the U.S. and Mexico.

One reason that the United States was suddenly so keen to annex Texas was because of the perceived threat from Britain. The British had benefited from tariff-free trade with Texas, importing vast quantities of cotton. Furthermore, Great Britain had outlawed slavery in 1833 and U.S. democrats feared that Britain would influence the Texan stance on slavery, perhaps forcing Texas to ban it. The threat of a black-protecting British colony bordering the slave-holding southern states was too much for the Democrats to bear. They believed that if Texas was to be annexed by any nation, then it ought to be the United States.

Log Cabin, New Braunfels, c. 1853, by Carl G. von Iwonski. The majority of colonists lived near small towns on farms like the one depicted here. (Daughters of the Republic of Texas Library at the Alamo)

Mexico did not concur. The United States had recognized Mexican Independence shortly after the revolution from Spain, yet the U.S. had not supported Mexico during the Texian War and had even allowed more Americans to cross the Sabine to foment revolt against the legal government. The Americans replied that the Texians, while being largely Anglo-Saxon and from the U.S., had merely succeeded in a revolt (a Mexican civil war) against the centralists' usurpation of the federal constitution, and that the republic had kept its liberty for almost a decade. The Americans also added that several key leaders of the Texian War of Independence were native Mexicans. This reasoning did not impress the powers of Mexico.

The Mexican general belief was that the northern United States had dispatched agents of insurrection to steal the territory from the rightful owners, and annexation was the final straw. They neglected to mention that the U.S. had recognized the Mexican Republic when she became independent of Spain.

Regardless, the Mexicans would view any attempt at annexation as an act of war. They communicated as much through diplomatic and other channels repeatedly during the early 1840s. On May 14, 1845, the Mexican Senate issued a report:

"1st. The Mexican nation convokes all her sons to the defense of the national independence, menaced by the usurpation of the Texan territory attempted by the decree of annexation given by [the U.S.] Congress and sanctioned by the President of the United States of the North.

2nd. Consequently the [Mexican] government shall put under arms all the force of the permanent and active militia, in conformity to the authorization conceded to

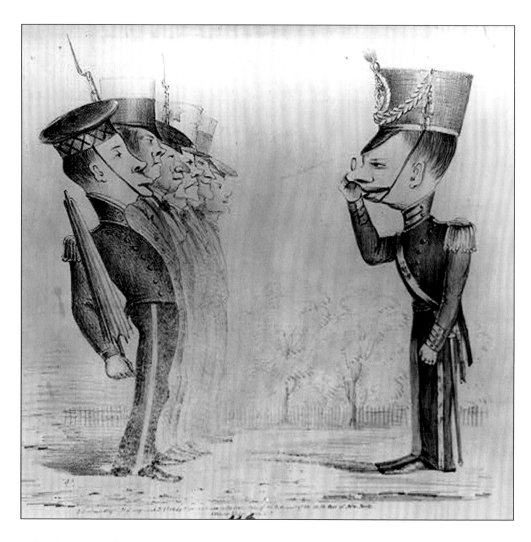

Volunteers for Texas, a scornful depiction of the volunteers who mustered to defend Texas against Mexican invasion in 1848. When news of Gen. Zachary Taylor's initial engagement with Mexican troops near the Río Grande first reached Washington on Saturday, May 9, many men flocked to support the popular cause by enlisting in the army. Most had no military experience and the artist shows an ill-equipped group of men mustering before an equally clueless officer who has failed to spot that the most prominent weapon among them is actually an umbrella. (Library of Congress, Prints and Photographs Division LC-USZ62-1272)

it, by the existing laws; for the preservation of Public order, support of the institutions, and in case of necessity, it shall employ the army as a reserve: & exercising the power conceded to it...it shall raise the forces mentioned therein, under the name of defenders of the independence and laws."

This was similar in language to other missives the Mexicans had produced and would produce up to the eve of the U.S.–Mexican War. Regardless, Texas was annexed as the 28th state to the United States on December 29, 1845.

On January 3 General Mariano Parades y Arillaga succeeded in his revolt against the government of President-General José Joaquin de Herrera and proclaimed that he would, "defend the integrity of the national territory ...every foot of Texas to the Sabine."

With his envoys and plenipotentiaries rejected by the Mexican government, on

June 15, 1845, Polk ordered Zachary Taylor with three brigades of regulars to Corpus Christi, Texas, as an Army of Observation. They remained at the mouth of the Nueces until March 8, 1846, when they marched south along the coast road (the same one Urrea had used a decade before) and into the disputed territory. On March 19 the Americans reached the Arroyo Colorado and were met by a messenger from the Mexican government. Capitan José Barragán (Santa Anna's escort commander during the Texian War of Independence) dared the Americans to cross, knowing that this would precipitate war. Taylor answered that he would begin crossing immediately. The large Mexican force, of which only a few cavalry were seen, withdrew without contesting the crossing.

Taylor arrived on March 28 and established operations on the Río Grande overlooking Matamoros, Mexico. He immediately set about constructing a star-shaped, six-sided fort with walls 9 ft (2.7 m) high and 15 ft (4.6 m) thick, surrounded by a moat. He also established a major supply base at nearby Point Isabel. His "army of observation" had become an army of occupation.

On April 12 Gen. Pedro de Ampudia was named commander of Mexican forces in the north and believed the Americans could be defeated in "four days." He also informed the American consul at Matamoros, "that an ... order would be given in respect to the Americans residing in the other towns on the frontier, and that all Americans who may be found to have passed to the left (Texas) bank of the [Río Grande] River, shall be shot within an hour after [being] taken."

On April 25, 1846, a 1,600-man Mexican cavalry brigade, augmented with a battalion of assault engineers and the 2nd Light Infantry, crossed the Río Grande and attacked, then captured 63 dragoons of companies B, C and F, 2nd U.S., commanded by Capt. Seth Thornton at Rancho Carricitos. The U.S.–Mexican War had begun.

With a large force of Mexicans across the Río Grande, Gen. Taylor grew concerned over his line of communication with Port Isabel. On May 1 he marched to protect his supply depot, leaving two batteries of artillery and the 7th United States Infantry in the new "Fort Texas." Leaving the fort, Taylor said the place would be renamed after the first officer to die defending it.

On May 3 the Mexicans laid siege to the fort and continued until May 7 with the acting commander of the 7th U.S. Infantry, Maj. Jacob Brown, being mortally wounded on May 6. The fort, and the town of Brownsville, Texas, still bear his name.

Taylor heard the artillery from Point Isabel and countermarched to break the siege. With his small force of regulars and Texas Militia, Taylor attacked and defeated the Mexican forces over two consecutive days at Palo Alto and Resaca de la Palma on the northern bank of the Río Grande. The Mexicans retreated across the river and Taylor pursued. By February of 1847, in less than nine months, Taylor had defeated the Mexicans in the northern states and United States forces controlled all key towns and roads. In a dramatic step, General Winfield Scott took a large portion of Taylor's army and invaded the Mexican port of Vera Cruz as Cortez had done centuries before. With this thunderclap invasion he defeated the Mexican army in Mexico City (once again under Santa Anna) and "conquered a peace."

Mexico not only "lost" her former territory of Texas, but a majority of the American southwest as well. Concurrent with rebellion in Mexico's northern colonies, Alta California was also in disagreement with the central government in Mexico City. Just as the Europeans were after Texas, they were even more enamored of California. The United States did not desire the European threat on the southern and, potentially, western borders.

The Treaty of Guadalupe Hidalgo was signed on February 2, 1848. Texas, New Mexico, Arizona, Alta California and portions of other future states were ceded to the United States.

Santa Anna would become president one more time and immediately sold the southern areas of present-day Arizona and New Mexico to the United States. These

45,535 square miles (117,935 sq km) of Mexico provoked another insurrection and Santa Anna left the pages of history.

The colonists with their roots in northern Europe won the war for control of the North American continent and control the territory to this day. The demographic is changing, however, as more Hispanics are moving into the U.S., legally—and illegally. It might not be too much longer before a *reconquista* takes place and the southwestern United States in culture, ethnic make-up and language again becomes the domicile of the former Iberians.

This lithograph depicts General Zachary Taylor's victory at the battle of Buena Vista on February 3, 1847. (Library of Congress Prints and Photographs Division LC-USZC4-6127)

Glossary

ambuscade An ambush.

bivouac A temporary camp without tents or cover.

Caddo A member of a group of Native American peoples of Louisiana, Arkansas and eastern Texas; the language of the Caddo peoples.

coatee A type of military coat that was cut away sharply in the front and had short tails in the back.

cockade A rosette or knot of ribbons worn in a hat as a badge of office.

détente An easing of hostility or strained relations, especially between countries.

dysentery Infection of the intestines resulting in severe diarrhea with the passage of mucus and blood.

fandango A foolish or useless act or thing; a lively Spanish dance usually performed by a man and a woman to the accompaniment of guitar and castanets.

farrier A craftsman who trims and shoes horses' hooves.

filibuster A person engaging in unauthorized warfare against a foreign country.

foment To stir up or instigate.

freebooter A lawless adventurer.

hegemony Leadership or dominance of one group or authority over others.

ignominious Deserving or causing public disgrace or shame.

jacales A hut in Mexico and southwestern United States with a thatched roof and walls made of upright poles or sticks covered with mud or clay.

junta A military group that rules a country after taking power by force.

kith and kin A phrase meaning one's friends, acquaintances and relations.

Law of April 6, 1830 A law initiated by the Mexican minister of foreign relations to stop the deluge of immigrants coming to Texas from the United States. It was one of the laws that helped propel the Texas Revolution.

nominal Existing in name only.

parochial Having a limited or narrow outlook or scope.

plenipotentiary A person, especially a diplomat, invested with the full power of independent action on behalf of his or her government, generally in a foreign country.

reconnaissance A military observation of a region to locate an enemy or find out strategic features.

scum A worthless or contemptible person or group.

shako A stiff cylindrical military hat with a brim, high crown and plume.

six pounder Also known as 6-pdr. (2 kg) cannon, a type of gun that was a common field artillery piece.

sutler A person who followed an army and sold provisions to the soldiers.

Texian Anglo (English-speaking American) citizens of Texas during the time when Texas was part of Mexico, before the United States annexed the Republic of Texas. After U.S. annexation of Texas, the term "Texan" replaced "Texian" in general usage.

vernacular The language or dialect spoken by the ordinary people in a particular country or region.

viceroyalty A district that is governed by a viceroy, someone who represents a sovereign in a colony, region or country.

vociferous Shouting in a noisy and insistent way.

For more information

The Alamo
P.O. Box 2599
San Antonio, TX 78299
(210) 225-1391 ext. 14
Web site: http://www.thealamo.org
The Battle of the Alamo is recounted at the
historic Alamo site, along with a history
of the mission.

Bob Bullock Texas State History Museum
P.O. Box 12874
Austin, TX 78711
(512) 936-8746
Web site: http://www.thestoryoftexas.com
This museum explains the history of Texas—
educating visitors about the land, identity
and peoples of the region.

Fannin Battleground State Historic Site
P.O. Box 224
Fannin, TX 77960
(512) 463-7948
Web site:
http://www.visitfanninbattleground.com
A Texas Historical Commission property, the
Fannin Battleground honors the brave
soldiers who fought the Battle of Coleto
Creek in 1836 during the Texas War of
Independence.

Fort Bend Museum
500 Houston Street
Richmond, TX 77406-0460
(281) 342-6478
Web site: http://www.fortbendmuseum.org
The museum preserves historical buildings
and artifacts relating to early Texas
history, including archaeological sites
around Richmond.

George Ranch Historical Park
10215 FM 762

Richmond, TX 77469
(218) 343-0218
Web site: http://www.georgeranch.org
The park provides programs to teach the
public about Texas history, including
the Texas War of Independence.

Handbook of Texas Online
Texas State Historical Association
1155 Union Circle #311580
Denton, TX 76203-5017
(940) 369-5200
Web site: http://tshaonline.org
This Web site is the "digital gateway to Texas
history." The online content includes in-
depth information on the Texas War of
Independence.

Republic of Texas Museum
c/o Daughters of the Republic of Texas (DRT)
510 East Anderson Lane
Austin, TX 78752
(512) 339-1997
Web site: http://www.drt-inc.org/
museum.htm
The museum is located at the DRT
headquarters, and houses more than
3,000 artifacts from the time of the
republic.

Sam Houston Memorial Museum
Box 2057
Huntsville, TX 77341
(936) 294-1832
Web site: http://www.shsu.edu
The Web site offers a timeline of
Houston's life and contributions to
Texas history.

Texas Historical Commission
P.O. Box 12276
Austin, TX 78711-2276

(512) 463-6100
Web site: http://www.thc.state.tx.us
The state agency for historic preservation,
    the organization works to preserve the
    architectural, archeological and cultural
    landmarks of Texas.

Texas Military Forces Museum
P.O. Box 5218
Austin, TX 78763
(512) 782-5659
Web site:
http://www.texasmilitaryforcesmusum.org
This museum's collections include artifacts
    on the militia and volunteer units relating
    to Texas military forces from 1823 to the
    present.

Texas State Library & Archives Commission
1201 Brazos

P.O. Box 12927
Austin, TX 78711-2927
(512) 463-5455
Web site: http://www.tsl.state.tx.us
This collection safeguards the Texas
    Declaration of Independence and other
    Texas documents and treasures concerning
    the Texas Republic and Texas history.

Web sites

Due to the changing nature of Internet
links, Rosen Publishing has developed
an online list of Web sites related to the
subject of this book. This site is updated
regularly. Please use this link to access
the list:

http://www.rosenlinks.com/eaw/tex

For further reading

Barr, Alwyn, *Texans in Revolt: The Battle for San Antonio, 1835*, University of Texas Press, Austin,1991.

Davis, William C., *Three Roads to the Alamo: The Lives and Fortunes of David Crockett, James Bowie and William Barret Travis*, HarperCollins, New York, 1998.

Fehrenbach, T.R., *Lone Star: A History of Texas and Texans*, Wings Books, New York, 1991.

Hansen, Todd, ed., *The Alamo Reader: A Study in History*, Stackpole Books, Mechanicsburg, Pennsylvania, 2003.

Hardin, Stephen L., Ph.D., *Texian Iliad: A Military History of the Texas Revolution*, University of Texas Press, Austin, 1994.

Harrigan, Stephen, *The Gates of the Alamo: A Novel*, Alfred A. Knopf, New York, 2000.

Huffines, Alan C., *Blood of Noble Men: The Alamo Siege and Battle, an Illustrated Chronology*, Eakin Press, Austin, 1999.

Jackson, Jack, *The Alamo: An Epic Told from both Sides*, Paisano Graphics, Austin, 2003.

Jackson, Jack (ed.), and John Wheat (trans.), *Almonte's Texas: Juan N. Almonte's 1834 Inspection, Secret Report & Role in the 1836 Campaign*, Texas State Historical Association, Austin, 2003.

Montaigne, Sanford H., *Blood Over Texas: The Truth About Mexico's War with the United States*, Arlington House Publishers, New Rochelle, New York, 1976.

Moore, Stephen L., *Eighteen Minutes: The Battle of San Jacinto and the Texas Independence Campaign*, Republic of Texas Press, Dallas, 2004.

Nelson, George, *The Alamo: An Illustrated History*, Aldine Press, Uvalde, 1998.

Ragsdale, Crystal Sasse, *Women and Children of the Alamo*, State House Press, Austin, 1994.

Schwarz, Ted, *Forgotten Battlefield of the First Texas Revolution: The Battle of Medina, August 18, 1813*, Eakin Press, Austin, 1985.

Shiffrin, Gale Hamilton, *Echoes from Women of the Alamo*, A W Press, San Antonio, 1999.

Stephens, A. Ray, and William M. Holmes, *Historical Atlas of Texas*, University of Oklahoma Press, Norman,1989.

Thompson, Frank, *The Alamo: A Cultural History*, Taylor Publishing, Dallas, 2001.

Todish, Tim J., and Terry S., *Alamo Sourcebook 1836: A Comprehensive Guide to the Alamo and the Texas Revolution*, Eakin Press, Austin, 1998.

Winders, Richard Bruce, Ph.D., *Sacrificed at the Alamo: Tragedy and Triumph in the Texas Revolution*, State House Press, Abilene, 2004.

Index

Agustin I *see* Iturbide, General Agustin de
Alamo, the 8
Alamo, battle of the 34–36, 37–44, 71–72
    Mexican retreat after 75–77
Alamo Presidial Company 31
Almonte, Colonel Juan 60–64, 84
    journal of 62
Ampudia, General Pedro de 87
Apache tribe 7–8
April 6 Law, the 19, 21, 23
Army of the People 24, 32
Army of Three Guarantees 17
Arredondo, General Joaquín de 11, 17
Austin, Moses 17
Austin, Stephen Fuller 17, 18, 22, 24, 32
Aztecs 6, 8

"Babe of the Alamo" *see* Dickenson, Angelina
Barragán, Captain José 87
Bastrop, Baron de 17
Bellows, Peter 74
Béxar *see* San Antonio de Béxar
Béxar, battle of 32–34
Bocanegra, José Maria de 84
Bonham, James 42
border distinctions 82–84
Bowie, James 26, 32, 34, 35, 36, 39
Bradburn, Colonel John Davis 19, 22, 45
British commercial interests in Texas 69–70, 84
Britton, James 74
Brooke, Fort 67
Brownsville, Texas 87
Burnet, David Gouverneur 24, 48, 62, 77, 78, 81, 84
Bustamente, Anastacio, President of Mexico 19,
    21, 60, 64

Camp Moultrie, Treaty of 66
Castañeda, Lieutenant Francisco 31
Castrillón, Major-General Manuel Fernandez y 26,
    40, 55, 57
Cavelier, René Robert 70
Childress, George Campbell 47–48
Clinch, General 67
Coahuila State 17, 23, 82
Collingsworth, Captain George 32
Comanche tribe 7–8
Cordoba, Treaty of 17
Coronado, Francisco Vásquez de 6
Cós, Major-General Martín Perfecto de 23, 26–27,
    32, 33, 35, 55, 75
Crawford, Jos. T. 69–70
Crockett, David 35, 40, 65, 71

Dade, Major Francis L. 67
Dade's Massacre 67, 69
Dickenson, Almeron 71, 72
Dickenson, Angelina 71–74
Dickenson, Susannah 71–74

Eastern Interior Provinces 17
El Camino Reale march 34–36
Elliot, Charles 69

Fannin, Colonel James Walker 26, 32, 34, 41, 47,
    49, 50, 51, 52
Filisola, Major-General Vicente 26, 44, 75, 76, 77, 79
Florida 66–67, 69
France 7
Franciscan order 7
French commercial interests in Texas 70

Gaona, General 42, 45
Goliad
    battle at 49–52
    massacre of Texians at 51–52
Gonzales, DeWitt colony 31, 32, 52, 71
Gray, William Fairfax 47
Griffith, John 74
Guadalupe Hidalgo, Treaty of 87
Guadalupe Victoria 50, 51, 75
Gutiérrez de Lara, Bernardo 10

Herring, Francis P. 74
Hidalgo y Costilla, Father Miguel 8, 10
Holmes, Oscar 74
Houston, Sam 22, 24–25, 34, 48, 50, 52, 53, 54,
    55, 57, 58, 59, 65, 75, 77, 84

Incas 8
Iturbide, General Agustin de (Agustin I) 17

Jack, Patrick C. 22
Jackson, Andrew, 7th President of the United States
    65–66, 84

Kemper, Samuel 11
Kennedy, William 69
King, Fort 67

La Bahía 11
Lamar, Mirabeau Bonaparte 82, 84
land ventures (*encomienda*) 7
Louisiana 7

Madrid, Treaty of 17
Magee, Augustus 10–11
Manifest Destiny, concept of 65
Martínez, Governor Antonio María 17
Mayas 8
Medina, battle of the 11
Mexican Army 29–30
    retreat after Alamo battle 75–77
Mexican independence
    and Agustin de Iturbide (1821) 17
    and Santa Anna (1823) 17
    war of 19, 21
Mexico
    abolition of slavery 21
    border distinctions 82–84
    and immigration 17, 18, 19, 21
    internal federalist wars 84
    invasion of Texas (1842) 82
    political sentiments 82
    status of under Spain 17
Mexico City 17

Milam, Ben 33
Mission Refugio 49, 50
Mission San Antonio de Valero 7, 8
Mission San Francisco de los Tejas 7
Monroe Doctrine 65
Montoya, Colonel 45
Morelos y Pavón, Father José María 60

National Convention, Washington Town 47–48
Navarro, José Antonio 82
Neill, Colonel James C. 32, 34, 35, 54
Núñez, Álvar 6

Oñate, Juan de 6

Palo Alto, battle at 87
Parades y Arillaga, General Mariano 86
Payne's Landing, Treaty of 66
Polk, James K., 11th President of the United States
    65, 84
Portilla, Colonel Nicolas de la 51

Ramírez y Sesma, General 42, 44, 47, 52, 53, 77
ranches (estancia de grando) 7
Republican Army of the North 11
Resaca de la Palma, battle at 87
revolt against Spanish rule (1810–1813) 8–11
Ross, Captain J.E. 78
Rubíl, Marqués de 7
Rusk, Thomas Jefferson 48, 58, 63–64, 77, 79
    funeral oration to Alamo fallen 79–81

Salcedo, Manuel María de 11
San Antonio de Béxar 7, 8, 11, 17, 31, 32, 34, 35,
    37, 71
San Jacinto, battle of 55–59, 75
Santa Anna Perez de Lebron, Antonio López de,
    President of Mexico 11, 87–88
    and Mexican independence 19, 21, 22, 23
    rise to power of 17
    and Texian War of Independence 26, 34, 37, 40,
    43, 44, 47, 51, 52, 54, 55, 57, 58, 59, 60, 64, 75,
    76, 78, 79, 81
Scott, General Winfield 87
Seminole Indians 66–67, 69
Seminole war, 2nd 69
Seven Golden cities of Cibola, legend 6

Sherman, Sidney 54, 79
slavery 84
Smith, Erastus "Deaf" 55, 72, 75
Smither, Dr. Lancelot 31
Spain
    conquests 5–8
    and Mexican colonial government 17

Taylor, Zachary 87
Terán, General Manuel de Mier y 19
Texas (Tejas) 6, 7
    and annexation by United States 84–88
    border distinctions 82–84
    chronology of War of Independence 12, 14–16
    colonists revolt (1832) 22
    political sentiments 82
    status of under Mexico 17–18, 27
Texian Republic
    and annexation by United States 84–88
    independence of 82–84
Texian Republican Army 27, 29, 53, 55, 56, 69, 72, 79
Tocqueville, Alexis de 65
Travis, Lieutenant-Colonel William Barret 22, 26,
    32–33, 35, 36, 37, 39, 40, 43
Trespalacios, Don José Felix 60
Turtle Bayou Resolutions 22

Ugartechea, Colonel Domingo de 22, 31
United States
    and annexation of Texas 84–88
United States—Mexican War 86
Urrea, General José de Cosme de 27, 34, 42, 44,
    49, 50, 51, 64, 75, 76

Velasco, battle of 22
Velasco, Treaties of 26, 78–79, 82
Viceroyalty of New Spain 6–8
Victoria, Guadalupe, President of Mexico 19

Wahoo Swamp, battle of 67
Washington Town 47–48
Williams, John 74
Wool, General 82

Zacatecas State 23, 82
Zavala, Lorenzo de 24, 25–26, 48
Zuñi tribe 7

About the authors

Professor Robert O'Neill is the series editor of Early American Wars. His wealth of knowledge and expertise shapes the series content and provides up-to-the-minute research and theory. Born in 1936 an Australian citizen, he served in the Australian army (1955–68) and has held a number of eminent positions in history circles, including the Chichele Professorship of the History of War at All Souls College, University of Oxford, 1987–2001, and the Chairmanship of the Board of the Imperial War Museum and the Council of the International Institute for Strategic Studies, London, England. He is the author of many books, including works on the German army and the Nazi party, and the Korean and Vietnam wars. Now based in Australia on his retirement from Oxford, he is the Chairman of the Council of the Australian Strategic Policy Institute.

Alan C. Huffines received his BA in History from Midwestern State University and took an MA in History at Norwich University in Vermont. He is an active duty field grade combat arms officer and received the Bronze Star Medal in the Persian Gulf War. He is the author of the acclaimed *Blood of Noble Men: The Alamo Siege and Battle, an Illustrated Chronology*, and *A Pilgrim Shadow* as well as several articles on the Texas Revolution. He has provided historical consulting work on feature films and documentaries.